T0323592

# Cambridge Elements ☰

Elements in Religion and Monotheism
edited by
Paul K. Moser
*Loyola University Chicago*
Chad Meister
*Affiliate Scholar, Ansari Institute for Global Engagement with Religion,
University of Notre Dame*

# ANGELS AND MONOTHEISM

Michael D. Hurley
*University of Cambridge*

CAMBRIDGE
UNIVERSITY PRESS

Shaftesbury Road, Cambridge CB2 8EA, United Kingdom

One Liberty Plaza, 20th Floor, New York, NY 10006, USA

477 Williamstown Road, Port Melbourne, VIC 3207, Australia

314–321, 3rd Floor, Plot 3, Splendor Forum, Jasola District Centre,
New Delhi – 110025, India

103 Penang Road, #05–06/07, Visioncrest Commercial, Singapore 238467

Cambridge University Press is part of Cambridge University Press & Assessment,
a department of the University of Cambridge.

We share the University's mission to contribute to society through the pursuit
of education, learning and research at the highest international levels of excellence.

www.cambridge.org
Information on this title: www.cambridge.org/9781009565318

DOI: 10.1017/9781009374644

First published 2024

*A catalogue record for this publication is available from the British Library*

ISBN 978-1-009-56531-8 Hardback
ISBN 978-1-009-37462-0 Paperback
ISSN 2631-3014 (online)
ISSN 2631-3006 (print)

# Angels and Monotheism

Elements in Religion and Monotheism

DOI: 10.1017/9781009374644
First published online: December 2024

Michael D. Hurley
*University of Cambridge*

**Author for correspondence**: Michael D. Hurley, mdh32@cam.ac.uk

**Abstract:** While angels have played a decisive role in all the world's major religions and continue to loom large in the popular religious and creative imagination, modern theology has tended to ignore or trivialise them. The comparatively few scholarly works on angels over the last century have typically interpreted them as mere symbols and metaphors: they are said to offer glimpses not of the divine order, but of human desires, anxieties, and ideologies. Angelology has collapsed into anthropology. By contrast, this polemical Element argues for the indispensable importance of studying angels as divinely created beings, for theology at large, and for understanding the defining doctrine of monotheistic religions in particular. Additionally, the Element contends that the spirit of modern science did not originate with the so-called Scientific Revolution but was actually inspired centuries earlier by the angelological lucubrations of medieval scholastics.

**Keywords:** angels, angelology, disenchantment, scientism, monotheism

ISBNs: 9781009565318 (HB), 9781009374620 (PB), 9781009374644 (OC)
ISSNs: 2631-3014 (online), 2631-3006 (print)

# Contents

A.M.D.G.

# 1 How to Write about Angels

The world was once aflush with angels, until they became irrelevant, if not embarrassing, and were almost completely exiled by the twin forces of secularism and scientism – almost, but not quite. Pockets of religion and popular culture remained hospitable, and over the last few decades, there has been something of a revival of interest within religious studies, New Age practices, literature, and the imaginative arts. Still, we are a long way from the historically high periods of angel veneration, far less their serious study.

Angelology's claim to be a systematic body of knowledge, announced in its suffix -λογία and attested through a long tradition of learned inquiry, is out of step with the academic conventions of our times. No longer 'queen of the sciences', theology has learnt to trim her ambitions – clip her wings, if you will – disavowing what James Joyce once called 'the true scholastic stink' (Joyce 2003, 214), along with the supposedly primitive elements of supernatural faith on which such studies were founded. Speculation on the angelic hierarchy that fascinated the likes of Pseudo-Dionysius and Maimonides, or Avicenna and Shihab al-Din al-Suhrawardi, has been consigned to its pre-modern oubliette.

It might be objected that there is today still a busy industry of books and articles on angels, and there is, especially Christian. But a closer look reveals that contemporary angelology is by no means what it once was; it has fundamentally changed its character. For the most part, across the Abrahamic faiths, the study of angels has become a zombie discipline, a revenant that staggers along without an authentic metaphysical life. The subject cannot be said merely to have evolved, because that would imply an organic relation to its former self, when it has in fact been travestied, in two directions.

On the one hand, it has been attenuated into fideism. Popular publications, the majority share of the market, are confessional, and insofar as they explain the nature and function of angels, they do so without pretending to academic rigour or systematic treatment. To say so is not to doubt the sincerity or even the veracity of such publications; it is only to observe that they stand on their own terms, as personal testimonies, substantially unaccountable to previous scholarship. Relatedly, 'one of the features of the contemporary upswing in interest in angels is that the formally non-religious are often happier talking about them than those who are part of a religious institution' (Stanford 2019, 8). Belief in angels is indeed often promoted without a corresponding belief in God.[1] Supernatural comfort is thereby promised without the corollary obligations

---

[1] 'A distinctive feature of the angels of the nineties, high as well as low, is their dissociation from orthodox religious contexts and their affiliation instead with other metaphysical phenomena

that come with a Supreme Being. This trend is not so much towards polytheism (a rebooted version of the pagan gods) as it is a kind of decapitated monotheism, to which Socrates long ago provided the appropriate riposte: 'what human being would believe that children of gods exist, but not gods?' (Plato 2017, 27A–28A).

On the other hand, angelology has collapsed into anthropology. Scholarly works typically treat angels not as objective ontologies, but as mere symbols and metaphors. By this praxis, angels do not offer glimpses of the divine order but of human desires, anxieties, ideologies. Celestial cathecting is said to extend from benign wish-fulfilment to our darkest sublimations, and of the 'range of ideas that we want to project', mortal isolation is usually judged to be uppermost: 'a need for this life not to be everything', for 'there to be something in that space between earth and sky', because 'we just didn't want to be alone' (Stanford 2019, 29, 46).[2] Even within conservative and evangelical circles, compared with earlier centuries there has been a dearth of 'serious discussion about angels' as divinely created beings (Potter 2017, 3).[3]

Such disenchanted talk is taken up especially when it comes to explaining the recent resurgence of angels in popular culture, which Harold Bloom has interpreted as a kind of 'populist poetry', said to have been precipitated in 1990 by Sophy Burnham's *A Book of Angels* (Bloom 2007, 4, 59).[4] Sundry claims have been advanced for this angelic comeback, everything from 'the tumbling of the [Berlin] Wall and the political change in 1989' to their serving as 'tools for imaginatively confronting the AIDS epidemic that was then ravaging gay communities', or as 'metaphors for mediation and information flow in an era of light-speed communication' (Serres 1995, 154; Wolff 2007, 695; McHale 2017, 43). Angels, by this reckoning, might as well be vampires, aliens, or ghosts – anything unreal and otherworldly: the effusion of human creativity, without any meaningful relationship to objective reality, or to any particular religious tradition.[5] They are an intellectual crutch and an emotional comfort-blanket in a puzzling and hostile world, a sheer confection for coping with 'the unbearable loneliness of our cosmic existence' (Wolff 2007, 695).

---

and violations of physical law – with ghosts, hauntings, and unsanctioned miracles' (McHale 2017, 35).

[2] Recent studies in the same vein include: Jones (2010), Bloom (1996), and Bloom (2007).

[3] For a survey of 'Gaps in Modern Angelology', from the limitations of Karl Barth's *Church Dogmatics* to the New Age movement, see Potter (2017, Ch. 4).

[4] On the return of angels in popular culture, see McHale (2017); also, Wolff (2007): 'No one reckoned with the comeback of angels about the turn of the millennium' (695); 'The great theologians of the 20th century had simply forgotten them or were ashamed of them' (695). Also see Wolff (1991).

[5] For a recent perspective on reinterpreting historical encounters with angels as possible encounters with aliens – while suggesting that both may be confabulations anyway – see Pasulka (2019).

But what if angels actually exist?

That innocent question deserves its own paragraph: its implications are immense and define the direction of this entire Element. Ask after the objective reality of angels, a question that historically never needed to be asked, and modern scholars are liable to smirk if not sneer at the possibility, which they prefer to dismiss in advance, and on first principles. That 'angels always turn up in times of crisis' (when, say, a religious cult loses its attractiveness, or a political system becomes unstable) does not itself tell us whether they are real or fantasised. For those open to the existence of angels, their resurgent popularity could equally be 'A sign that the saving power is approaching in apocalyptic danger' (Wolff 2007, 695). Crises may be a catalyst for delusive projection, in other words, but crises would also presumably be the occasions when real divine intercessors, if they really existed, would be most likely to intervene.

Contemporary angelology is in any case unable to adjudicate on such questions, because it has boxed itself into an epistemological corner. Caught between fideism and anthropology, it struggles to reconcile religious conviction with scholarly respectability. Although it is possible to express one or the other, it proves difficult to entertain both at the same time. The reasons for this are far reaching and express the extent to which modernity has conceived of faith and reason as antagonistic modes of knowledge; or, at best, 'non-overlapping magisteria'.[6] More will be said on this as it pertains to angels in Section 3. It is sufficient to note here that while the epistemological problem faced by angelology is being immediately pinned to modernity, for reasons that will be teased out in what follows, it was actually incipient from the very beginning.

The existence of an invisible world composed of good and bad spirits was universally acknowledged from the earliest stirrings of the Abrahamic faiths. It could hardly have been denied, given the prominence of spiritual creatures throughout the holy books on which those faiths were founded. Scripture raised more questions about these spirits than it answered, though, such that it was necessary, as Joseph Turmel observed in his 1898 history of angelology, to resort to 'la conjecture philsophique ou aux raisons de convenance théologique' (Turmel 1898, 407). That meant going beyond exegesis, to consult also the evidence and logic of Church and cultic traditions, as well as prior and analogous theological positions, together with private prayer, contemplation, and reason.[7]

---

[6] Advocated by Stephen Jay Gould (1997) and (1999). For a recent Islamic perspective by a similar rationale, see Guessoum (2010).

[7] Even Pseudo-Dionysius, who founded his angelology on biblical exegesis, ultimately looked beyond Scripture, at times contradicting it: see Peers (2001, 4–5). Islamic angelologists who define angels as incorporeal find themselves contradicting several clear statements in the Qur'an to the effect that angels have material substance: see Burge (2012, 99).

The more elaborately such supra-Scriptural speculations are unfolded, however, the more contestable they may become. Anna Jameson spoke for many in 1848 when she cavilled at the ways in which, taking for their basis only 'a few scripture texts', 'the imaginative theologians of the Middle Ages ran into all kinds of extravagant subtleties regarding the being, the nature, and the functions of the different orders of angels' (Jameson 2012, 45).

At once accountable to Scripture, but at the same time prompted by Scripture to rely on other sources: Turmel and Jameson address the perennial bind faced by angelology. And yet there is also a sense in which their responses are inflected by a peculiarly modern prejudice. Both authors make their remarks in the contexts of celebrating the existence of angels. So their prejudice is not like that of, say, William Robertson Smith, whose entry on 'Angel' in 1875 for the ninth edition of the *Encyclopaedia Britannica* likewise considers the 'Biblical data' on angels to be 'very scanty', but who – unlike Turmel and Jameson – goes on to raise questions about whether angels are any more than the 'poetic art' of the human imagination (Smith 1875, 26–28). When Jameson speaks of the 'extravagance' of medieval theologians, she is not quibbling with their belief in angels (she shares that same belief), only the lavishness of their taxonomies. Turmel strikes a similarly belittling note when he portrays the enterprise of angelology with the language of scholarly self-indulgence, as a desire to 'contenter la curiosité' (Turmel 1898, 407).

There is, to be fair, something judicious in both assessments. Angelology is a subject for which Scripture only offers a prologue, and it is easy to see how the opinion might form that the scholastics really should have circumscribed their studies accordingly. The trouble is that angelology is too important to be so circumscribed; it cannot be dismissed as a speculative sideshow. The theological stakes are much higher than this. Look to the seminal interventions on the subject across millennia, and angels are regarded as an essential constituent of the religious cosmology at large. They are not studied as a private whim, but as an indispensable feature of a complete metaphysics, and one that represents real and important knowledge: 'curiosity' does not cut it.

Jameson and Turmel are not cited here because they demonstrate how belief in angels is wavering within the nineteenth century; that point could be made more forcefully by piling up further examples like Smith, who was accused or heresy soon after his article on angels and other religious subjects appeared in the *Encyclopaedia Britannica*. Jameson and Turmel represent something more intriguing, something crucially different. They suggest how far even scholars who believe in angels are, since the nineteenth century, liable to downplay their significance in ways that are at odds with the longer history of angelology; ways that are instead consistent with the modern historicisation of religion in general. While diminishing the scholarly standing of angelology, curling a lip at its claims to knowledge, may look like something very different from disbelieving in angels, religious history shows that the former attitude inevitably reflects and nurtures the latter. Scepticism about angelology leads to scepticism about angels.

'The fact that religion is a fully cultural construct is fairly evident', writes Maurizio Bettini: 'if it weren't, its practices and organization would not have changed so radically from one era to another, from one continent to another, or from one nation to another' (Bettini 2014, 3). This chain of reasoning is familiar within modern discourse on religion, but it turns on a simple fallacy, obscured by Bettini's use of 'fact' but belied by his subsequent qualifications, 'fairly evident' and 'so radically'. 'Fairly' concedes that the evidence is not definitive; 'radically' begs the question of whether a given religious evolution is extrinsic, expressing merely outward cultural trappings, or intrinsic, referring to a 'root' change.[8]

The importance of this distinction between extrinsic versus intrinsic change can hardly be overstated; it touches a foundational assumption of angelology. Put most directly: religious doctrine may develop while remaining coherently true. The contingencies of human experience across different times and cultures do not necessarily discredit the truth of a given faith; they may actually create the conditions in and through which its truth most fully emerges. G. K. Chesterton glossed the principle with characteristic limpidity:

> When we say that a puppy develops into a dog, we do not mean that his growth is a gradual compromise with a cat; we mean that he becomes more doggy and not less. Development is the expansion of all the possibilities and implications of a doctrine, as there is time to distinguish them and draw them out [. . .]. (Chesterton 1933, 7)[9]

That the human understanding of angels has been informed by human history, experience, and nature, and that some salient claims within angelology remain unresolved, does not, by this logic, perforce exclude the possibility of their objective existence. Competing accounts of angels might also, as part of an authentic doctrinal development, suggest the limited and shifting human capacity to construe them. These are not exclusive possibilities. Contradictory

---

[8] Originally written in Italian, Bettini's use of the word 'root' will be even closer to the Latin etymology of the English word 'radical' that, like the late twentieth-century theological school of Radical Orthodoxy, assumes the logic of recovery rather than mere reinvention.

[9] For the classical articulation of this principle, see John Henry Newman's *An Essay on the Development of Christian Doctrine*, which was originally published in 1845 (Newman 1878). For a contemporary thesis as it relates to the Islamic rather than Judeo-Christian tradition, see Guessoum (2010).

and changing opinions may express the conflicted and shifting perspectives and circumstances of human experience, but they may also – not as an alternative, but as a concurrent possibility – reveal the abiding fallibility of human beings.

Dante Alighieri tips a wink here, reminding us that even great popes and saints may err when determining the divine order. Gregory the Great is said to have laughed at himself ('di sé medesmo rise') when he made it to heaven and realised his mistaken ranking of the angelic hierarchy (Dante 2007, 28.133–35). Dante implicitly includes himself in this humbling, since he had previously followed Gregory's system, rather than what, in the *Commedia*, he now presents as the true order contemplated by Dionysius the Areopagite. From top to bottom: Seraphim, Cherubim, Thrones, Dominions, Virtues, Powers, Principalities, Archangels, and Angels (Dante 2018, 2.5.6).

As was common in the Middle Ages, Dante was unaware that the works issued as if by Dionysius were in fact written by the fifth-century Christian Neoplatonist who has come to be known in the contemporary world as Pseudo-Dionysius. But the principle stands. Dante makes no special claim for Dionysius *qua* scholar: the canto ends by explaining that mortal man was not able to access such hidden truth through rationality alone, but only because it was revealed to him (Dante 2007, 28.136–39).[10] Pseudo-Dionysius had himself already made the same contention, contextualising what it is angelology can authoritatively claim to know through reason, by presenting knowledge of divine things as something that only fully reveals itself through the 'truly mysterious darkness of unknowing' (Peers 2001, 5–6).[11] For all the confident precision of angelology, it is irrefragably provisional.

This is where things, from an academic perspective, become awkward. Appealing to the necessity of revelation and the limits of reason is all very well in certain poetic or religious contexts, but modern scholars are not so easily satisfied by this move. Pope Leo XIII closed his intervention on epistemology after the Enlightenment, *Aeterni Patris* (1879), by enjoining the faithful to 'follow the example of the Angelic Doctor', Saint Thomas Aquinas, 'who modestly confessed that whatever he knew he had acquired not so much by his own study and labour as by the divine gift' (Leo XIII, §33). In religious terms, it was a potent and needful intervention. But advocating a return to Scholastic philosophy that can integrate faith and reason does not readily translate into the professionalised academic world: it is an affront to method. Where the encyclical urges 'modesty' when it comes to knowledge acquired by

---

[10] For an illuminating discussion of this passage, see the commentary in Dante (2007, 166–67).
[11] Quoted in Gill (2014, 17). Gill elaborates the point as it applies to visual depictions of angels. For an account of Dionysius's angelology, see Perl (2007).

reason and empirical inquiry, the modern academy has challenged the legitimacy of knowledge conferred through divine gift.[12] Hence the secular historicisation of angelology.

Thankfully, this trend has not been universal. Within the Christian tradition of writing about angels (more will be said in due course about Judaism and Islam), two interventions stand out for their theological trenchancy – one from the twentieth and one from the present century: Sergius Bulgakov's *Lestvitsa Iakovlia: Ob angelakh* [*Jacob's Ladder: On Angels*] (1929), and Serge-Thomas Bonino's *Les Anges et les Démons: Quartorze leçons de théologie catholique* [*Angels and Demons: A Catholic Introduction*] (2007). In framing its material, the first, *Jacob's Ladder*, is presumptively assertive:

> It goes without saying that the doctrine of angels is not only of scientific-theological but also of religious-practical interest for every Christian. (Bulgakov 2010, xiii)

The second, *Angels and Demons*, is more concessive:

> I have no trouble admitting that the teaching about angels and demons is not the heart of the Christian faith. This is a side issue, a marginal teaching about a peripheral truth in the hierarchy of revealed truths. (Bonino 2016, 1)

The difference between these starting positions is not as stark as it at first appears. Bonino offers a lengthy footnote where the quotation given above leaves off, in which he clarifies that the existence of a hierarchy of revealed truths – an objective, logical order among the truths taught by the Church – 'in no way implies that the secondary truths are optional in the eyes of faith': 'All of them must be believed with supernatural faith' (Bonino 2016, 1, fn. 1). Bulgakov nonetheless remains the more strident, and with some cause. His systematic treatment of the role, meaning, and purpose of angels is informed not only by Scripture, liturgy, icons, and the Western and Eastern patristic traditions, but also by his own miraculous encounter with an angelic presence.

*Jacob's Ladder* is indeed an astonishing intervention and is self-consciously part of a celebrated angelogical tradition that includes Dante's exemplar, Pseudo-Dionysius, as well as Saints Aquinas and Augustine.[13] But comparing Bulgakov's book with studies on angels from an earlier age also highlights a key difference. Pseudo-Dionysius, Aquinas, and Augustine each share Bulgakov's conviction that angels are of central importance for 'every Christian', and to be regarded as such both in 'scientific-theological' and 'religious-practical' terms.

---

[12] For a revealing account of this papal encyclical in the context of the development of what counts as rational knowledge, see MacIntyre (1990).

[13] See Potter (2017, Ch. 3) and Klein (2018).

Their convictions are implicit, however, and did not therefore need to be pressed. They were in that sense men of their respective times and cultures, where Bulgakov stands athwart his milieu, and (like Leo XIII) he knows it. 'It goes without saying' is in the end the surest way of indicating that something does in fact need to be said. Once more, Chesterton offers a keen distillation of the principle:

> Real history, if there could be such a thing, would not consist of what men did, or even what they said. It would consist far more of the mighty and enormous things they did not say. The assumptions of an age are more vital than the acts of an age. The most important sentence is the sentence that a whole generation has forgotten to say; or felt it needless to say. (Chesterton 1990, 21, 446)

While Bulgakov's and Bonino's works are, then, continuous with the distinguished tradition of angelology, they are also – Bulgakov reveals implicitly, Bonino explicitly – works of remembering what has now been largely forgotten. They address what newly needs to be said. Something definitive has changed in the metaphysics of angelology between their studies and those on which they are founded. Of the many examples that might illustrate this change, Henry Mayr-Harting's 1997 lecture on *Perceptions of Angels in History* is especially suggestive, for the ways it is, and at the same time is not at all, self-conscious about its presumptions. The lecture opens with Mayr-Harting describing his appointment to the Regius Professorship of Ecclesiastical History at Oxford as breaking with 'tradition'. He is referring to the fact that he is Roman Catholic rather than an Anglican. But the substance of his Inaugural Lecture reveals a far more severe break with tradition that goes entirely unremarked, presumably because it seemed entirely unremarkable.

From the pulpit of one of the most prestigious Chairs of theology in the world comes a lecture on angelology that disavows a belief in angels. More than this: Mayr-Harting questions even the relevance of holding such a belief for angelology as a discipline. 'Angels are comparatively little studied these days,' he observes, 'except by people interested in the paranormal, which I am not' (Mayr-Harting 1998, 2). The untheological lexicon here is deliberate; 'paranormal' has an intellectual priggishness about it, as against the more respectable, ready-made religious alternative, 'supernatural'. With a witty dash of what E. P. Thomson called 'the enormous condescension of posterity', belief in angels is rendered superstitious from the outset (Thompson 1963, 12). For good measure, the apparently incidental qualifier, 'which I am not', makes it urbanely obvious that the lecture to follow will suffer no such nonsense.

'Yet angels have always played a strong role in the religious sense of the great monotheistic religions': Mayr-Harting concedes the importance of angels for religious believers while casting doubt on the credibility of that same belief (Mayr-Harting 1998, 2). He cites the 'highly reputed anthropologist', M. J. Field, whose *Angels and Ministers of Grace* (1971) influentially argued that all the angels of the bible must have been human beings, or else those who claimed experience of them were hallucinating, or both (Mayr-Harting 1998, 3). The thesis that follows is even more devastating. We are advised that it does not matter if angels exist or not anyway. The question of their reality should be suspended indefinitely, the argument goes, in favour of asking something more productive; namely, 'what is the point or function of perceiving certain experiences or apparitions as angelic or otherworldly?' To prioritise this concern is to assume 'It matters little whether angels occur in visions or waking life; what matters is their function in the event or storyline' (Mayr-Harting 1998, 4). But it does in fact matter, and not a 'little', whether the angels under inspection have a life of their own beyond our projections and misprisions. To assert otherwise is to be profoundly at odds with the 'tradition' of angelology to which Mayr-Harting's lecture seeks to contribute.

Not that there ever was a single 'tradition'. Angelology establishes itself across different religions and times, and is typified by ongoing refinements, challenges, revisions. Nor was there a golden age of settled faith on angels, any more than we are now in an age of universal scepticism. Debates have always been contentious, and included clashes between the authoritative, primary sources (typically, Scriptural) versus folk and cultic traditions and practices, versus the reasoned interpretations of philosophy and theology.

Pseudo-Dionysius, for instance, averred that only archangels and angels, the lowest orders of his hierarchy, meet with human beings, which leads him to re-interpret Isaiah's encounter with the Seraphim (Isaiah 6:6) somewhat symbolically. The Seraphim in question were, he says, really common or garden angels (Roques 1958, lxxviii–lxxix). Such a case of mistaken celestial identity is, though, different in kind from suggesting that *all* encounters with angels are explicable as a kind of human error. When, say, Islamic angelologists define angels as incorporeal, and find themselves contradicting several clear statements in the Qur'an to the effect that angels do in fact have material substance,[14] that is a different order of theological wrangling from the rejection of the ontology of angels as such, which is the default assumption of modern angelology. The sea-change in theology over the last century or more has led to a situation in which to write about angels requires scepticism about the foundational truth of the subject itself.

There are, as noted, some doughty exceptions, and more examples will be given in due course. Nonetheless, the overwhelming tendency is that exemplified

---

[14] See footnote 6.

by Mayr-Harting. To take a comparable example from Judaism, Mika Ahuvia's *On my Right Michael, on my Left Gabriel* (2021) is a wonderfully erudite and incisive work of scholarship on its own terms, but it is also characteristically quick off the mark with its desacralising disclaimer. Before the book even gets going, before any misunderstanding can take root, the author's ambition is defined for the reader in terms of what it is not: 'This work makes no ontological claims as to the existence of angels' (Ahuvia 2021, 9). Even within Islam, where belief in angels forms one of the pillars of the religious system (Alavi 2007, 5–42), of the same standing as belief in God and the prophets,[15] scholars routinely reduce angels to more and less helpful figments of the imagination.[16]

Angelology has always asked hard questions of itself. Disagreement is par for the course; it is what propels the discipline. Aquinas argued that the existence of angels could be inferred from the idea of a perfect universe, whereas Ockham viewed it as a matter of faith: a profound difference.[17] Their dispute never extended to a denial of angels, however, nor to their importance for understanding the place of human beings within the divine scheme. That is a modern incitement. When Philo of Alexandria connects what Greeks call *daimons* with what Jews and Christians call angels, he is wary of being mistaken for relativising the truth of his subject, and so confronts this potential misapprehension directly: 'let no one suppose that what is here said is a myth' (Philo 1929, 2, 499).

The case of a fiercely independent thinker like Thomas Hobbes is helpful here, for underscoring just how different contemporary scepticism about angels is from earlier deliberations. Hobbes admits he is not minded to believe in them at all, but finds his hand forced:

> Considering therefore the signification of the word Angel in the Old Testament, and the nature of Dreams and Visions that happen to men by the ordinary way of Nature; I was inclined to this opinion, that Angels were nothing but supernaturall apparitions of the Fancy, raised by the speciall and extraordinary operation of God [. . .] But the many places of the New Testament, and our Saviours own words, and in such texts, wherein is no suspicion of corruption of the Scripture, have extorted from my feeble Reason, an acknowledgment, and beleef, that there be also Angels substantiall and permanent. (Hobbes 1651, 214)[18]

Insofar as Hobbes believes in Christianity, he feels compelled to believe in angels too, on the evidence of revelation given within that religion's holy

---

[15] It was cited in the case of Naṣr Abū Zayd: see Burge (2012, 226, n. 4).

[16] Islamic modernist scholars who have reinterpreted angels allegorically and metaphorically include Muhammad Asad and Ghulam Ahmed Parwez: Guessoum (2010, 50–51, 168).

[17] See Iribarren and Lenz (2008, 6).

[18] For a discussion of this quotation, see Ross (1985, 509).

book.[19] Contemporary theologians feel no such compunction. Where Hobbes is chastened by his own 'feeble Reason', the *eidos* of modernity presumes the opposite. The script has been flipped. Today, feebleness of mind is assumed to be the curse of credulity afflicting those who take angels to be real.

Maimonides, a towering philosophical figure, undermined the enthusiasm for angel veneration within Judaism, by rationalising and depersonalising them, turning them into natural forces and intelligences:[20] 'while he gives the Hebrew term *malakh* many meanings, the one he refuses to attach to it is that of a being with independent, continued existence, sent on missions by God and visible to human beings' (Kellner 2006, 272–73). Still, even he did not come close to calling them delusions. While he was surely revolutionary among Jews of his time for rejecting the anthropomorphised conception of angels found in rabbinic midrashim, liturgical poetry, and mystical texts (building instead on Hellenistic philosophical trends),[21] and while his treatises on angels do appear to have influenced others to demote their conception of angels accordingly, it is telling that his approach 'is much more influential today than it was in his own day or throughout the medieval period' (Ahuvia 2021, 214). 'Until the twentieth century most Jews lived in a world full of angels' (Ahuvia 2021, 214). Since that date, in the words of the 1908 *Jewish Encyclopaedia* entry on angels, such a belief has come to be glossed as a 'highly fanciful' notion from which Judaism should finally seek to liberate itself (Blau 1906).[22]

This historical shift is explicable as a function of modernity's secular-minded scientism, but it also reflects an increased awareness of how angels have been conceived differently across different times and places. That is a smoking gun for constructivists like Bettini, who jump from the commonplace that cultures differ and change to the assumption that angelology is nothing more than the passive expression of that change. When it comes to how angels have been understood and depicted, important variations certainly do emerge over the centuries within different religions, and even within the same religion. Accounting here only for the major monotheisms that are the subject of this Element, it is in that sense fair to say that 'there is no "Jewish angelology", "Christian angelology," or "Islamic angelology" that one can speak of; but rather, each faith has a range of "angelologies" that changes from text to text

---

[19] Hobbes is a suggestive example for the fact that he evidently had misgivings about his faith, and was known to do so, to the extent that the House of Commons in 1666 would cite his atheism as the cause of the fire and plague of London. See Wood (2012, 242). For a discussion of the emergence of atheism and its relations to the Enlightenment, see Eagleton (2014, 1–43).

[20] See Maimonides, *Mishneh Torah, Hilkhot Yesodei Ha-Torah* 2:3–8; *Guide for the Perplexed* 2:6.

[21] See Ahuvia (2021, 213). See Kellner (2006, 285): 'Maimonides' world, relative to that of many of his rabbinic contemporaries, was demythologized, de-ontologized – in a word, de-paganized'.

[22] Quoted in Ahuvia (2021, 214–15).

and theological stance to theological stance' (Burge 2012, 52). As a subject, angelology can therefore easily look like a hopeless free for all, with no stable content. But the story is not in the end so simple. Much will be said on this score in what follows. For now, priming the next couple of sections that argue for the integrity and importance of the discipline, two essential counter-considerations may be trailed: the extent to which angels elude human understanding; and the extent to which speculating about angels serves wider theological aims. These will each be tackled separately, but they must ultimately be seen together, as a way of reconciling the paradox that while angels can be conceived in contradictory ways, these contradictions may also, in the final analysis, cohere.

Angelology faces a further, deeper paradox that this Element also explores, as it pertains to monotheistic religions in particular; to wit, that angels are both necessary and perilous to monotheism's defining doctrine. Without angels, God is simply too far away to be known or loved, and yet angels also threaten the idea of a Supreme Being in the first place. This is metaphysics wagered on a razor's edge. Venerating spiritual creatures, even recognising that such creatures exist, risks reducing God to 'the status of a tribal deity' (Davies 1973, 51, 243).

## 2 How to Estimate Angels

Quite when and why angels fell from favour is a consequential and possibly ironic point. The standard narrative charts their decline from the Scientific Revolution of the sixteenth and seventeenth centuries, when the new clockwork certainties of physics and cosmology had 'no room in them for angelic intentions' (Fox and Sheldrake 1996, 12). Newton's paradigm-shifting discoveries were moreover compounded by Descartes' complementary revolution within philosophy, which transformed the whole method of philosophical inquiry so as to begin not with metaphysics but with epistemology.[23] The new broom of Protestantism was stiffened by this emergent Newtonian-Cartesian worldview, as it sought to clear out practices said to be superstitious and idolatrous, as well as the mediation of religious authority and worship deemed unnecessary and obstructive. With the Reformation came the idea that, like the priestly hierarchy on earth, the celestial hierarchy might, and perhaps should, be circumvented by those seeking an authentic relationship with God.

---

[23] 'After Descartes, angels had no place in a mechanistic universe' (Rees 2013, 55). Several centuries after Descartes, Newman diagnosed the legacy of this Cartesian shift: when it comes to religious belief, including a belief in angels, leading with the language of 'logic' is doomed from the outset: 'its chain of conclusions hangs loose at both ends; both the point from which the proof should start, and the points at which it should arrive, are beyond its reach; it comes short both of first principles and of concrete issues' (Newman 1870, 272).

Revolutions in science, philosophy and religion all played their part in squeezing the numinous from the world, then, and the effect on angels was palpable. Once awesome creatures were tamed into prettifying ornaments in the ensuing centuries, emasculated and infantilised into cute, chubby cherubs. Not all was lost all at once. There was a vibrant persistence of angel adoration in certain religious quarters, and evidence of brilliant thinkers, not only theologians but leading scientists too, still looking to angels as a source of knowledge. This is hardly surprising given the extent to which, it turns out, the leading scientists and philosophers of the early modern period were themselves thoroughly implicated in the medieval worldview their work presumed to supersede. Newton was an alchemist as well as a physicist, and heavily influenced by Rosicrucianism (White 1999, 117), which held to the specially chosen ability to communicate with angels or spirits. Descartes drew on what Aquinas and Duns Scotus say about angels in his account of the human mind and the nature of human knowledge and was more influenced by the reality as well as the idea of angels than he cared to admit (Scribano 2015, 17). Father of analytical geometry and modern philosophy he may have been, but he was also by his own account inspired to 'lay the foundations of a new method of understanding and a new and marvellous science' by the 'Angel of Truth' who appeared to him in a series of dreams (Maritain 1944).

Effused through chapels, shrines, prayers, poems, sculptures, stained glass, coins, clerical vestments, and pilgrim badges every bit as much as the writings of the great scholastics, the Middle Ages was surely the hey-day for Christian angelology, as it was for Judaism and Islam too, which laboured to see angels in terms of Aristotelian cosmology. Marvelling at this peak for celestial lucubration and devotion, it is easy to exaggerate the rate and extent of its subsequent decline. The historical record shows that angelology in fact continued in lively ways for centuries after its supposed death knell. The study of angels does not actually reach its nadir till the beginning of the twentieth century, at the juncture when, as Virginia Woolf famously announced, something within 'human character' itself seemed to have 'changed' (Woolf 1966, 1, 320).

Woolf is describing, amongst other things, what the contemporary philosopher Charles Taylor has explained as a movement from a 'porous' to a 'buffered' self; that is, from being open to the experience of a spiritual world that impinges on the human to one that is effectively bounded by its material horizon (Taylor 2007, 539). Science becomes the *bien pensant* worldview, both doxa and dogma, while religious knowledge is routinely stigmatised as regressive. 'I am not saying that one went out, as one might into a garden, and there saw that a rose had flowered, or that a hen had laid an egg': Woolf is quick to circumscribe her claim, even while she insists on its brute fact: 'But a change there was, nevertheless; and, since one must be arbitrary, let us date it about the year 1910' (Woolf 1966, 1, 320).

Woolf spoke from the heart. She found the idea of believing in God in the early twentieth century to be 'shameful and distressing', even 'obscene', though that may have been because she suspected human character had not in the end changed as much as she had hoped (Woolf 1997, 3, 475–78). Something certainly changed, and dramatically; but once again, spirituality was by no means extinguished.

Stephen Pinker is amongst those who have argued that the rise of the scientific worldview is not a matter of switching one epistemology for another. Religious and scientific perspectives and practices are, he is keen to stress, different in kind. The former is what he calls 'magical thinking', whereas the latter trades in what is verifiable (Pinker 2018, 5). But science today is by no means the enterprise of Newtonian causality that he pretends it to be. Relativity and dark matter, chaos and quantum: unexpectedly, modern science has enabled once more the pre-modern perspective of thinking about the world as constitutively strange and mysterious and unpredictable. Which all makes for a provoking riddle: as science has, in principle, become more compatible with angelic life, why have angels become less tenable within scholarly discourse? One answer was offered by Hilaire Belloc, who was every bit as shrewd as Woolf in assessing the mirror logic to her disenchantment. Science, he lamented in an essay of 1928, had not so much displaced as it had replaced the reflexive fealty of primitive religion:

> There never was such a time as our own for the use of magical words divorced from reason and used as talisman. I think the worst of all is the word 'Scientific.' It is used with a force of finality as though, once used, all discussion ended. A thing having been said to be established 'Scientifically' there is no more questioning of it. An opponent having been proved unscientific is out of Court. [. . .] The word is used like the name of a tribal god, to overawe an Opponent [. . .]. (Belloc 1931, 203)

It is tempting at this juncture to conclude, with Bruno Latour, that we have never really been 'modern', not in the seventeenth century, not in the twentieth, and still not now (Latour 1991). But is the de-mythologising conceit of modernity itself really a myth?[24] Disenchantment certainly appears to co-exist with a boom in certain forms of spiritual faith. Look beyond Newton and Descartes to other luminaries associated with the birth of science and the evidence quickly stacks up on the side of spirituality, including angelology, exemplified by a

---

[24] For rich discussion on this topic see Josephson-Storm (2017).

figure like Dr John Dee, eminent mathematician and scientist, astronomer to Queen Elizabeth I, who published hundreds of conversations he had personally enjoyed with angels.

Modernism likewise, for all its *soi-disant* rationalism, was an epoch that saw great popularity for spiritualism and the revival of magical orders like the Golden Dawn. Nor was this activity a freakish sublimation by a religious-minded remanent. Marie Curie, one of the very few people to win two Nobel prizes (physics and chemistry) was an avid participant in séances (Josephson-Storm 2017, 1–2). The adage that no man is an atheist in a foxhole took on a specifically angelic inflection in the Great War, with an upswing in battle-ground sightings, most famously documented as the Angels of Mons, who were said to have protected the British Army from defeat by the invading forces of the German Empire in Belgium on 23rd August 1914.[25] As so often with angels, the evidence inevitably cuts both ways. Those sceptical of the existence of spiritual creatures take wartime visions to be proof that psychological projections surge in times of trauma; those who believe in the possibility of angels counter that they have long been known to fight with human beings (see Figure 1).[26]

As for our fractious postmodernity, while institutional religion continues to decline, spirituality continues to find new outlets, through the re-mixing of ritualistic, personal, and political practices, from the revival of witchcraft and Gwyneth Paltrow's gospel of Goop, to SoulCycle and those communities who believe in their special destiny on Mars (Burton 2020). Whether or not these expressions of what William James called 'the religious impulse' should be counted with religions proper is beside the larger point that the current moment is by no means fully convinced of the secular-materialist assumptions that supposedly define it (James 1920, 507). The world's major monotheisms have in any case been unwittingly complicit in diverting the spiritual appetite of the modern world into these dubitable outlets, insofar as they have shied from affirming their own metaphysical identities, downplaying their more substantial spiritual traditions and beliefs in favour of ethical and cultural commitments. This turn away from metaphysics to ethics is especially apparent within first-world Christianity, the religion of the Abrahamic faiths that has historically expended more theological energy on angels than Judaism and Islam combined.

As John Cottingham has described it, far from being bullish about the super-natural requisites of their faith, far even from wrestling with doubts about those requisites, 'the typical Anglican clergyman or woman of Great Britain,

---

[25] See Davies (2018) and Ruickbie (2018).

[26] On war-time support from angels, see Gitta Mallasz's 88 conversations with angels that took place in Hungary towards the end of WWII (1943–4), published as *Die Antwort der Engel* (Einsiedeln 1981).

**Figure 1** A depiction of Muhammad (with veiled face) advancing on Mecca from Siyer-i Nebi, a sixteenth-century Ottoman manuscript. The Prophet and his companions are attended by the angels Gabriel, Michael, Israfil, and Azrail. Siyer-i Nebi: The Life of the Prophet 1595. Hazine 1223, folio 298a.

particularly at the upper educational end (Oxbridge chaplains and theology fellows, for example) [. . .] are perfectly calm and comfortable about, for example, rejecting miracles like walking on water, or the feeding of the five thousand, at least on anything like a literal interpretation' (Cottingham 2015, 79). The doctrine of the Incarnation is likewise up for grabs; so too the Virgin Birth, the historicity of the Christmas narratives of the wise men and shepherds, even the locus of Christ's birth itself, Bethlehem (the consensus being that he was born in Nazareth). Only the Resurrection, perhaps, is safe from the long march of demythologisation, at least for now.[27] Within such a compromised religious culture, angels are amongst the first things to go. In Islam, despite the importance placed on angels in the process of revelation (its sense of 'delivered' revelation is stronger than is readily found in the Bible or the Jewish and Christian traditions), a number of modern thinkers have culled them. Talk of angels as divine emissaries is said to be misleading, if not plain silly. The important 20th century theologian Fazlur Rahman rejects the notion of Gabriel as divine 'postman', which he argues to have only emerged in the eighth century. Revelation is reframed as a psychological and experiential act. As the Iranian theologian Abdolkarim Soroush would have it, 'the Angel Gabriel was part of Muhammad, or appeared in his imaginative faculty, and thus was not an external being vís-à-vís the Prophet' (Akbar 2020, 63).[28]

Extirpating angels is not a discrete act. It suggests and also abets a general movement towards demythologisation. Cutting out angels indirectly cut off God. This is true in the sense that, without mediation, God can simply feel too far away. But more subtly too, angels lend support to the very idea of a Supreme Being. This paradoxical claim, trailed already in the opening section, will be taken up most fully in the final section of this Element. Before that, something first needs to be said about the inherent as well as the heuristic value of angelology, for theology, but also, unexpectedly, for its two supposed disciplinary antagonists: philosophy and science.

Scepticism about the value of studying angels can often be just another expression of the philistinism that has always dogged philosophical inquiry, for which Plato's *Apology* rehearses the archetypal instance. Socrates indicted even unto death for wasting time searching for 'what's below the ground and in the heavens' is aptly transferred to angelologists (there can be no angelology proper without demonology too) (Plato 2017, 19b–c). Animosity towards the apparently intellectually outlandish – in the full sense of that word – finds fresh expression in every culture.

We are, though, also living in an exceptional time, in which organised religion has never been so derided. Pinker's brittle philippic against irrationality, *Enlightenment Now* (2018), is broadly representative of the contemporary conceit that would

---

[27] For an influential counter to the trend of demythologising Christianity, see Heiser (2015), which argues that the biblical narrative reveals a cosmic struggle between God and spiritual forces, making belief in the supernatural essential to the Christian faith. Heiser has also written on angels in particular (2018), arguing that they are integral to the biblical narrative and God's cosmic plan.

[28] This paragraph is indebted to Stephen Burge, who shared with me his unpublished but forthcoming entry on 'Angels in Islam' for the *St Andrews Encyclopaedia of Theology*, which closes with a discussion of the demythologising of angels in Islam.

dismiss all forms of religion under the same catch-all category of 'magical thinking'. Religious belief might like to think of itself as different in kind from superstition and occultism, but Pinker would have us see it as the same species of pre-scientific ignorance. The counter-objection bears repeating. Simply, that contemporary science is not sheerly positivist in its approach; it is not, in the final analysis, governed by deterministic certainties, but by 'freedom, openness and spontaneity' (Fox and Sheldrake 1996, 12, 13).[29] Mysteries that had been foreclosed by the earlier, more mechanistically minded eras of inquiry have been re-opened. New mysteries have also come into view. Through modern physics, Karl Popper once observed, 'materialism has transcended itself'; and the same might be said of modern biology and chemistry too. On angels in particular, there are fascinating parallels between how Aquinas figured angelic movement in the Middle Ages and how Einstein would describe photons in the twentieth century. (Fox and Sheldrake 1996, 23)

Whether or not angels can be tolerated within a modern philosophical and scientific worldview, there is work to be done to demonstrate the value of angelology as such. The cliché conundrum of the discipline concerns how many angels can dance on a pinhead. How could one ever know? More damningly, who cares anyway? Whether or not angelology is pseudo-scholarship, even if the questions over which it worries *could* be answered, it is not obvious why they matter in the first place.

Angelologists never actually turned their attention to angels dancing on pinheads. The story was invented by seventeenth century Protestants to mock mediaeval scholastics (Asselt 2011, 65). That the anecdote stuck is its own indictment, however. Satire only works if it approximates the truth it ridicules. There is after all an anonymous fourteenth-century mystical treatise, *Swester Katrei*, that refers to a thousand souls in heaven sitting on the point of a needle, and another disquisition around the same time on how many angels might fit within an eye of a needle.[30] It is not such a stretch to imagine angelologists testing the numerical limit with the added variable of performing rhythmical steps.

Another tale of angelology's self-indulgence tells of how, in May 1453, at the very moment in which Constantinople was falling into the hands of Turkish invaders, theologians gathered into the heart of the besieged city to debate the sex of angels. Historians disagree about whether this actually happened, but as with dancing on pinheads, it matters less that the story is apocryphal than that it is deemed *ben trovato*.[31] Looking only to my own back yard: it is hard to defend

---

[29] See also Sheldrake (2013).
[30] For a fuller discussion, see Ross (1985, 495), which cites this example as part of his discussion of the angels-on-pinheads anecdote.
[31] For an account of how angels were deployed artistically after the fall of the city, as a form of lament but also reconciliation, to 'circumscribe the new reality', see Karanika (2016, 248).

the intellectual energy expended by Dr John Worthington, Vice-Chancellor of the University of Cambridge in the seventeenth century, on the question of whether good angels could wear beards. That a university's senior leadership is disconnected from reality is, alas, a perennial complaint; but even with such depressingly low expectations in mind, Dr Worthington's interests seem embarrassingly abstruse (Ross 1985, 507).

That the study of angels is unimportant, edging towards risible, is a charge often endorsed by religious believers themselves, out of a kind of pragmatic savvy, from a fear that, in the contemporary climate, a religion which emphasises the spiritual dimension of existence lacks credibility. Moderation is the name of the game. Bonino distils the 'tactic' in vivid terms: 'establish that angelology is an extrinsic element and not part of the substance of revelation itself,' 'an option that can be scrapped without damaging the essentials', and then what is deemed 'essential' might have some chance of being taken seriously (Bonino 2016, 73). It is far from clear that this 'tactic' achieves its ambition. It is also unclear how far the marginalisation of angels within modern religion is in fact merely tactical, and how far it instead betrays ignorance about angelology's value, or scepticism about the supernatural character of religious faith more broadly.

On all counts, it is relevant to recall the 'tactic' of Ludwig Feuerbach's *The Essence of Christianity* (1841), which pursued its claim that 'theology is anthropology' – God is not an objective, transcendent reality, but a fictional human projection – under the pretence that seeing Christianity in this way would not diminish it, but on the contrary help to preserve it (Stewart 2020). The reverse came to pass, of course, and it moreover seems clear that it was Feuerbach's intention that this would be the case. It is well to learn the historical lesson.

That religion does not refer to an objective truth, that it is a human invention, has a much longer history than Feuerbach, obviously, going back at least as far as ancient Greece. There was nonetheless something seminal in Feuerbach's critique, which, drawing on Hegelian philosophy, and catching the wave of post-Enlightenment humanism, gained traction even within the schools of theology that would oppose it. And the compromised metaphysics of reading theology as anthropology continues to play out today. No doubt many modern theologians simply do not believe in angels. For those who do, the plan to cut out angelology in the service of saving the greater theological body has backfired. The reason is simple: angels are not like tonsils or wisdom teeth; they are more like vital organs. Remove them and the whole body fails. Angelology is, in Bonino's terms, 'essential' to the life and health of theology as a whole.

Aquinas, arguably the greatest of all Christian theologians, was one of its greatest angelologists too. His elevation to the status of the 'Angelic Doctor' recognised his vast contribution to angelology, but also to theology at large. More correctly, his angelology makes sense of his theology at large. The principle applies likewise in reverse. Pseudo-Dionysius is best known for his contributions to angelology, but the Dionysian corpus was second only to the Bible and the works of Boethius in the number of translations, editions, and further commentaries it generated throughout the Middle Ages and the early modern period, and its influence extended not only into theology in the broadest sense, as we understand it today. It had a very significant influence on the theorisation and practice of the humanities and of the sciences too.[32]

To render angelology as a piffling or periphery discipline is, in other words, to misread its genealogy, reach, and influence. Seminal interventions come not from obscure figures with eccentric interests, but from amongst the most prominent theologians, often when mediating between epochal civilisational changes during which discussion of angels plays an important role. Augustine is an obvious example to stand alongside Aquinas and Pseudo-Dionysius, straddling as he does the classical and the medieval world. Karl Barth is another, speaking to the modern Protestant tradition. Within Judaism, no less a figure than Maimonides devotes significant sections of his treatises to angels (Ahuvia 2021, 213–14).

Crucially, such distinguished theologians do not include a discussion of angels *as well as* other mainstream consideration of the religion; their angelology must be understood within, and makes fuller, finer sense of their complete theological corpus. The theological topography in which angels are to be found is part of an exhaustive metaphysical map. Questions of the status of angels as created beings, including but by no means limited to their corporeality, their knowledge, their free will, their peccability, their capacity for speech, and the quality of their song: what is determined about angels in these and many other domains bears on analogous questions applied to God, to human beings, and to the rest of creation. Angelology is the study of angels, but it is also simultaneously engages with a full gamut of metaphysical and noetic concepts, following the logic that angels can and should be understood by comparison and contrast with other beings within the hierarchy of being. It is by this logic that

---

[32] See Harkness (1999a, 107). John Marenbon suggested to me that this claim by Harkness must be exaggerated – that the volume of translations, editions, and commentaries on Aristotle would surely be more numerous, and perhaps the commentaries on the *Sentences* of Peter the Lombard too. However the numbers stack up, the Dionysian corpus, including his vision of angels, had a vast influence for many centuries, not only within niche corners of theology but very widely across the developing European intellectual landscape. Harkness cites Froelich (1987, 37–38).

angelology is said to be governed by 'thought experiments' (Perler 2008, 144).[33] When Scotus and Ockham discuss angelic cognition, they are motivated by an interest in the general structure of cognition even more than what is specific to, say, Gabriel or Raphael:

> They both wanted to know how cognition works in principle, i.e., what kinds of entities and relations are required in any cognitive process. An analysis of angelic cognition provides some kind of theoretical map that indicates the place and function of all the elements involved in a cognitive process. Once this map is drafted, it can be used not just as a guide to angelic cognition but also – and even more so – to human cognition. (Perler 2008, 152–53)

The relative standing of angels to human beings allows this reflexive turn, from angels to humans. Distinctiveness emerges out of the tension between similarity and difference. To know what a cat is, Bonino observes, there is nothing so like comparing it with another feline, such as a lion or a panther:

> Our ancestors, in order to understand better the specific nature of man, therefore compared and contrasted him with the angel, his cousin in the order of spiritual beings. Today the chimpanzee has replaced the angel in this role, and not to the benefit of the humanities. (Bonino 2016, 2)[34]

Bonino does not gloss what exactly is lost to the humanities by focusing on chimps, but one of the benefits of thinking about human beings through comparison with angels rather than apes is that it reveals what is distinctive about the Supreme Being believed to have created them both. In his text praising the Archangel Michael, Chrysippus (ca. 405–79) teases at both the similarities and also the differences in the natures of Michael and God (Peers 2001, 3). Angelology allows humans to gain conceptual purchase on a divinity otherwise defined by ineffability. Where the leap from human beings to God is beyond human capacities, angels provide a bridge. Angelologists frequently write of the example angels set for humans, notably when it comes to worship.

Apes, by contrast, direct attention away from what is spiritual towards our animal nature, to hunter-gathering, mating rituals, dominance behaviour, and so on. The locus shifts from intellect to instinct. There is clearly value in conducting anthropology via apes, given the close biological relationship. Thinking about apes may also perhaps correct the Neo-Platonic tendency of (especially medieval) angelology to think about human nature in ways that run counter to the incarnational theology of Christianity. Judaism and Islam also

---

[33] See also Bonino (2016, 2).
[34] On how medieval thinkers sought to understand human nature in comparison with angels, see Schumacher (2023).

face something of the same dilemma. In the Qur'an, when all the angels bow down to Adam except for Iblīs, Iblīs explains his refusal on the basis that a creature made of fire should not have to bow down to one made from mud (Qur'an 7:12; 17:61; 38:76). This episode generated much debate in the classical period, the most controversial view being that of the Sufi al-Hallāj in his Tāwasīn, where he argues that Iblīs was, to his credit, a perfect monotheist because he refused to prostrate himself before something that was not God.[35]

Unsurprisingly, whether or not angels take bodily form becomes a keenly important consideration for the chain of being: humans are more often said to be higher in the order than angels, not in spite of, but *because* they have a bodily as well as a spiritual form. However the arguments run, the spiritual nature of angels is not exclusive from their having a physical form, in both a narrow and wider sense. The narrow sense means that they might occasionally assume bodily form (this was insisted on in, for instance, the 1277 Condemnations).[36] The wider sense means that, even if they do not have bodies (conceived as pure energy, say, or light), they are nonetheless items to be accounted for in a scientific understanding of the universe – as indeed is every real thing, except for God, who accounts for rather than is accounted for. There can in any event be no angelology without a lucid sense of how angels compare with the rest of creation, and with humans most of all.

There is an arresting scene in Chesterton's nightmarish novel, *The Man Who Was Thursday* (1908), when we meet the 'anarchic poet' Lucian Gregory, described as 'a walking blasphemy, a blend of the angel and the ape' (Chesterton 1996, 9, 8). It is a macabre image, and an uncanny shadow of angelology. Aquinas marks the orthodox position: 'By their nature angels are between God and man' (Aquinas 2006, I-I, Q. 64, A. 4). What makes the image blasphemous in Chesterton's rendering is not that humans occupy a middle position between terrestrial and celestial, but rather the fact that his position is 'blended'. It ought to be clear, so that the differences might mutually correct each other. That is the animus of Aquinas's insight:

> Hence, the incorporeal substances are midway between God and corporeal things and the point midway between extremes appears extreme with respect to either; the tepid compared with the hot seems cold. Hence the angels might be called material and bodily compared with God, without implying that they are so intrinsically. (Aquinas 2006, I-I, Q. 50, A. 1)

---

[35] See Burge (2012, 10) and Awn (1983, 33–37).

[36] Which is not to say that angels have bodies, only that while being fundamentally intellectual and spiritual, they could potentially assume or interact with physical forms when necessary. This stance is consistent with Scriptural accounts where angels appear to humans in tangible forms.

More pointedly, that inveterate hedger Blaise Pascal once opined:

> It is dangerous to show man too clearly how much he resembles the beast, without at the same time showing him his greatness. It is also dangerous to show him too clear a vision of his greatness without his baseness. It is even more dangerous to leave him in ignorance of both. (Pascal 1960, 61, fragment 236)

The entire ambition of angelology, it might even be said, is just such a work of un-blending, as it were, man from beast and angel and God – while avoiding the antithetical blasphemy of insisting too fully, either, on the differences. Angels can only be a bridge between humans and God if they are understood to share something with both. Collapsing that distinction in either direction is disastrous for the metaphysics of monotheism. It scrambles the categories of what it means to claim that God is both transcendent and immanent. As will be explored more fully in the final section, angelology must be steered between the Scylla of entirely denying divine agency in the world through deism, and the Charybdis of dethroning divine sovereignty by misreading the doctrine of the univocity of being.

## 3 How to Learn from Angels

That 'angels provide privileged grounds for exploring a whole range of issues from epistemology and metaphysics to philosophy of mind and language' is an important first step to recognising the value of angelology as a discipline (Iribarren and Lenz 2008, 4). The study of angels is undersold, however, if it is treated as if it were merely what Shankar Vedantam and Bill Mesler have called a 'useful delusion' (Vedantam and Mesler 2021). Studying angels can certainly serve as a proxy for other kinds of inquiry: 'even in those arguments in which angels appear to be the prime focus (such as angelic hierarchies), the actual debate is often located elsewhere', such that 'many ideas about angels are the biproducts of theological disputes, cited, or perhaps created, to support other means' (Burge 2012, 107). What, though, if anything, might be the value of studying angels directly, *as* angels?

Constructivists aver that the recent revival of interest in angels is only a variation on the pop-cultural craze for cyborgs, or vampires, or zombies. 'Collectively', as Brian McHale has described it, 'these para-human types serve to define the fully human by their difference – their respective differences – from humanity' (McHale 2017, 44).[37] Angels do and do not fit this paradigm. Within the long arc of religion, angelic inquiry takes its force and mandate from the

---

[37] Also see Damon (1997, 206).

presumption that angels were actually believed to exist.[38] Accordingly, angelology cannot be reduced to 'a crypto-anthropology that any serious hermeneutic could show to be alienating and illusory in the final analysis'; nor can it be viewed as only a historical retrospect, 'the now-empty religious chrysalis in which the modern concept of the human subject was supposedly formed' (Bonino 2016, 3). If angels are nothing more than the projection of human subjectivity, they cannot perform their most basic and important putative function so far as human beings are concerned, which is to bring them closer to God's person and will.

'Only the ontological reality of the angelic world guarantees the reality of humanity's openness to something greater than itself' (Bonino 2016, 4). Taking angels seriously redirects anthropocentrism into theocentrism. Contemporary theology has abetted the anthropological turn as part of a general secularising drift in religious studies, but that drift has also been observable for some time. Contemporary theology frames discussions of God in ways that make the presence of God difficult to access;[39] it prefers to avoid angels altogether. But angels have always required a bold faith to speak about them, not least because they are for the most part, as Augustine allows, 'hidden from our eyes' (Augustine 2000, 103.1.15, 124). Where Augustine diverges from modern theology is that his concession to difficulty refuses to concede doubt: 'We hold this firmly, and it would be wrong for us to doubt it' (Augustine 2000, 103.1.15, 124). The boldness to believe in this way – seen through a glass, darkly – extends from angels to the entire metaphysical worldview of the Abrahamic faiths.

Sigmund Freud, no friend to religion (which he thought to be a neurotic illusion), was nonetheless incisive in his last book, *Der Mann Moses und die monotheistische Religion* [*Moses and Monotheism*] (1939), when he identified Judaism's greatest contribution to be the worship of an invisible God. That transformed the whole balance of civilisational focus from the physical to the spiritual. Christianity very obviously took up this legacy, as Islam would too: it is impossible to miss the stricture at the beginning of *Surat al-Baqara*, that followers 'believe in the Unseen' (Qur'an 2:3). But angels are not just another part of this religious imaginary that includes belief in the invisible. While angels are themselves difficult to fathom, they offer intimations of God's will and nature that otherwise confound human comprehension. Angelology at once expresses the arduousness of understanding angels, and at the same time the possibility of meeting the infinitely greater arduity of understanding God.

---

[38] AI is perhaps closing the comparison between cyborgs and angels, forcing questions about what is distinctive in human thinking, analogous to medieval debates on what makes angels intellectually different to humans. See Lenz (2008).

[39] For an extended account of how and why 'Modernity exists under the sign of absence', see Orsi (2016, 38; passim).

That some writers on angels also believe in them is not therefore an incidental fact. As a conceptual category, angels have an evident 'cash-value' (as William James would say) for explaining other things, but that currency changes if the category's referent has an objective existence. If angels exist then they exercise influence in the world, which alters the conditions for human moral agency, the nature of God, and the relationship between human beings and God. Such knowledge cannot be won purely in the spirit of 'let's pretend'.

To be clear, thought experiments are a potent means of pursuing knowledge, and angels or angel-like creatures have been deployed by philosophers very richly in just such a mode. Immanuel Kant did so freely, as did John Locke.[40] Angels are used within their philosophising as a means to an end, operating something like the square root of minus one: while the notion itself has no reality in the world, like any so-called imaginary number, the way it is wielded (by mathematicians, physicists, and engineers, and so on) can have concrete applications.[41] There is nonetheless a difference between thinking about angels as fictions rather than facts, suggested by the way that certain thinkers toggle between the two: 'belief in angels is integral to a central aspect of Leibniz's metaphysical system,' for instance, 'without which it would be unrecognizable' – yet he sometimes uses the concept of an angel to make a purely conceptual point: 'to emphasize the discursive nature of human reasoning', say, 'by contrasting it with the simultaneous awareness of premise and conclusion in the mind of an angel' (Ross 1985, 510).

What is distinctive in these different modes of inquiry turns not on how an angel is conceived (thought experiments determine their own limits), but rather on what that conception implies for the religious cosmology in which the angel features. Thought experiments pick up and put down angels to this or that instrumental purpose; their cash-value is cashed out in a very restricted way. By contrast, angelologists who take angels to be real cannot even speculate on the beating of an angel's wing without potentially causing a theological tornado somewhere else. That is because angels are understood to be an integrated part of a complete, divinely created order; even small tweaks to how we think of angels can therefore have vast consequences for other building blocks of the metaphysical system.

'Philosophy at its best has always striven to achieve a "synoptic" vision of reality, a "worldview" that, so far as possible, aims to make sense of the cosmos and of our human place within it' (Cottingham 2015, xi): what John Cottingham

---

[40] For a discussion of how these and other philosophers conjure with angels without requiring belief in their existence, see Ross (1985).

[41] Although imaginary numbers are not physically 'real', they are more than just 'fiction'; they have a form of existence in the same way that any mathematical objects do, and may also be interpreted metaphysically. On 'the miracle of the appropriateness of the language of mathematics for the formulation of the laws of physics', as 'a wonderful gift that we neither understand nor deserve', see Wigner (1960, 14).

describes for philosophy in general is keenly true for angelology. Scholars who study angels are not typically seeking discrete answers to localised questions. They are more like Walt Whitman's patient spider: 'Ceaselessly musing, venturing, throwing, seeking the spheres to connect them' (Whitman 1897, 343).

'Angelology is often seen as an outstanding example of the barren metaphysical speculations that, allegedly, characterised (late-) medieval thought, or, at best, as a rather arcane curiosity that might be of some interest to specialists in the history of mentality, but is embarrassing to philosophical commentators' (Goris 2003, 87). So writes Harm Goris in his robust defence of why even the topic of angelic speech (a comparatively unstudied subject within angelology, itself comparatively unstudied) is instructive for understanding Aquinas – his thought at large; and for understanding Augustine and Aristotle too, with whom he more and less explicitly engages on this question.

Similarly, when Augustine devotes almost the entire central section of *The City of God* to explaining how angelic, as against demonic, behaviour provides human beings with a direct example of the right relationship to God, he is not indulging a theological diversion, nor establishing a set of placeholders for the principles he wishes to advance. His angelology is not mere analogising. His account of spiritual beings who have agency and participate in our lives has implications that run across his cosmology. 'Augustine has been appropriated by many theologians and philosophers of the twentieth and twenty-first centuries in their efforts to understand Christianity's proper relationship to the modern state', Elizabeth Klein observes, with the rider that 'very few of the authors who take Augustine as their patron even mention angels and demons, despite their prominent place in the oft-cited *City of God*' (Klein 2018, 108). Such an approach is inadequate for anyone who wishes to construe Augustine's legacy in all its complexity:

> What does our political theology look like when we recognize that the two cities are not primarily made up of human beings? That is, what does a non-anthropocentric politics look like? This challenge does not merely pertain to the orientation of politics toward a final eschatological consummation of the cities in the future. The two cities, for Augustine, were founded by angels and demons, and are currently populated by them. (Klein 2018, 108)

That the mundane world is thrumming with spiritual beings has tremendous, inexorable consequences; and they cannot be ignored within Augustine's theology without impoverishing and misrepresenting his vision as a whole.[42] Barth's 'doctrine of angels', sometimes called 'the most important discussion

---

[42] See, for instance, Augustine's *Teaching Christianity* (Augustine 1996), which enjoins us to love all human beings, but also all angels, who are counted as our neighbours (*proximi*) (Augustine 1996, I, 30– 33); see Augustine (1996, I, 36), elaborating the implications of believing in angels not as mere abstractions, but as real beings, and in our midst.

of the theme in modern theology' (Pannenberg 1994, 103),[43] has been similarly neglected.[44] Barth is a salutary figure to think about in this respect, for writing against what he called 'the angelology of the weary shrug of the shoulders' (Bonino 2016, 96): the notion that we do not need an account of good angels to conceive of human goodness, nor fallen angels to understand the nature of sin and the consequences of misusing freedom; that we can understand both on their own terms and would indeed likely understand them better in that way.

Angelology is by that estimation an indirect way of expressing a theological anthropology that could be told directly. It is not merely superfluous; it is positively unhelpful. Why not dispense with the prolegomenal exercise, then, and cut from the baroque abstractions straight to the subject at hand? 'Away with these shadows!', David Strauss implores: 'Let us hold fast to the full, concrete life, to complete beings, complete personalities, and not to complete angels or devils, which are only half a personality and so no personality at all' (Strauss 1841, 18).[45] Barth's thundering response is worth quoting at length:

> Who would admit the accusation of superstition and fantasy because he talks of the true, the good, and the beautiful (or of error, evil, and ugliness) in the same grave, earnest tones in which a dogmatician speaks of the angel Michael and of Satan? Would we accept that concepts such as 'art', 'science', 'education', 'the fatherland', 'history', 'national character', 'state', 'law', 'humanity', 'proletariat', 'progress', 'the idea of leadership', 'the revolutionary principle', 'the youth movement' are empty constructions, castles in the clouds, in face of which we might well raise the call: back to concrete life! Would it be proper to draw the attention of the sober Americans to the fact that they were wrong to erect that famous statue in New York harbor to *freedom* rather than to the 'complete personality' of some one of their happy fellow citizens? [. . .] Mark it well: It will not do to protest against speaking in abstractions. Not only because one should avoid pedantry and should have a little fun and some taste for poetry and symbolism, but because we find it impossible to conceal the fact that symbols correspond all the way down the line with *realities*. (Barth 1985, 319–20)[46]

Barth's insight is needful to emphasise within the context of the modern religious imagination that struggles far more than, say, the medieval mind,

---

[43] See also Tavard (1968, 93): Barth undertakes 'the most significant theological attempt to renew angelology in Protestantism', and along the way offers 'the most consistent and thorough overview of an angelology in modern theology'. Both quoted in Wood (2013, 321).

[44] On how Barth's doctrine of angels has 'languished' – 'there remains to date no comprehensive study of Barth's angelology in any language' – but why it is important to the understanding of his theology as whole, see Wood (2013, 319, 321).

[45] For a fuller account of Barth's angelology, see Wood (2013).

[46] Eng. trans.: Barth (1991). Quoted in Wood (2013, 330–31).

to think about the reach as well as the limit of abstractions. There is today a tendency either to short-circuit to literalism or else to imagine that symbolic language means plain fiction. We have lost confidence in the possibility that language can, asymptotically, gesture to truths which otherwise resist propositional description, by non-literal, 'literary' means – from metonym to myth to metaphor. Turning the tables: the problem with abstraction lies with the modern sensibility rather than with abstraction itself. As the contemporary Iranian philosopher Sayyid Jalal as-Din Ashtiyani would have it, only interpreters 'unable to understand abstraction' render angels as 'birds functioning as postmen with many large wings' (Eshkevari 2012, 121, n. 65).[47]

Wood puts his finger on what all this might mean for angelology as a discipline when he observes that, in the doctrine of created spirits, 'we directly reflect upon the reality of that aspect or side of creation which is not directly amenable to our perception and control but that nevertheless genuinely impacts upon our lives; and we thereby come to understand something of the character of these non-quantifiable influences':

> Thus Barth claims that we do not 'postulate this alleged shadow-world' only as a rhetorical embellishment of a self-sufficient naturalistic account of the world, but 'we reckon intellectually and aesthetically' with the 'elemental principles of the world' (cf. Col 2:8) 'because we reckon with them *ethically* and *religiously*; that is, because we *respond* to them – always voluntarily – and because we "fear, love, and trust" them – though one hopes not "above all things"'. The principalities and powers are not, in other words, merely projections upon an ethically vacuous network of cosmic relations but 'spiritual movements and dependencies that follow their own laws' even if they never exist in total isolation from the natural-mechanical laws of the universe. (Wood 2013, 333)

So much hangs on whether or not angels are 'merely projections'. As emphasised above, to regard them as objective realities makes all the difference because it postulates their significance within a cosmology that is tightly joined up. To treat them as an expression of human subjectivity hitches their significance only to human experience; to regard them as God's creations is to understand them as part of a complete order that includes both the heavenly and human realms. What Sachiko Murata argues for Islam thus applies without qualification to Christianity and Judaism too: 'concepts of creation, revelation, prophecy, the events that occur in the world, worship, the spiritual life, death,

---

[47] The same reductive misreading of angels leads to anthropomorphising God as a king with a long beard on a throne, heaven and hell as literally above and below the earth; and so on.

resurrection, and the central position of man in the cosmos cannot be understood without reference to angels' (Murata 1987, 324).

How perverse, then, that angels today find themselves on the fringes of theological discussion. As a barometer for how bad things are, with the exception of S. R. Burge's extremely important contribution, *Angels in Islam* (2012), there has not been a single recent monograph on angels in Islamic thought. Angels have not simply been neglected; they have been neglected because they have also been trivialised, made into a contingent and optional feature of the human experience. That has drastically changed how we understand them. The pet pooch, tamed and trained to obey its own owner's every expectation, behaves very differently from the wolf on the prairie. Angelic domestication is widespread even within Islam, which of all the Abrahamic faiths is most prescriptive about the necessity of believing in angels, and at the same time, generally least subject to modern revisionism.

It a question of some nicety as to what remedial work might be done to restore the importance of angels within modern theology. A first precaution must be to draw red lines: not to concede too much ground to the secular presumptions of the modern academy. In Section 1, brief allusion was made to the way modernity has presented faith and reason as antagonistic or, at best, 'non-overlapping magisteria'. The best-case scenario here, influentially argued by Stephen Jay Gould, emphasises the spheres of scientific and religious inquiry as fundamentally distinct: the former trades in facts, the latter in values. Scientific and religious truths are not rivals, because they seek to address different questions by different means. There is surely something to be said for thinking in terms of this division of labour, but the proposed cut is in the end too clean and too deep.

Gould is keen to protect the legitimacy of religious truth. 'If religion can no longer dictate the nature of factual conclusions residing properly within the magisterium of science,' he notes, 'then scientists cannot claim higher insight into moral truth from any superior knowledge of the world's empirical constitution' (Gould 1999, 9–10). Splitting the difference in this way may seem sensible, but it delegitimises any claims that religions might wish to make about the objective nature of reality. And clearly, religions do routinely wish to make claims of that sort. When it comes to angels, scientific language and method may be invoked, even as angelologists insist that the higher spiritual knowledge ultimately resists human inquiry. Angelology is a science, but also exposes the limits of science; it offers glimpses of a splendour that it can never fully grasp.

When Marsilio Ficino reflected on the order of the angels, he expressed himself in mathematical terms. Each of the nine orders of angels contain many legions, and each legion consists of 'six thousand six hundred and sixty-six individual spirits, and there are as many legions in each individual order as there are individual spirits in a legion' (Ficino 1576, 14).[48] That yields a grand total of 44,435,556 spirit-beings per order, which makes 399,920,004 in all (Rees 2013, 45). If there is something reassuringly, arithmetically anchored about this approach, it is upset soon enough by Ficino's unwillingness finally to parse out the celestial hierarchy with such certainty. He agrees with Pseudo-Dionysius that the number of angels is actually so large that it is beyond human reckoning. His apparent contradiction forces a greater subtlety. The exactitude of the angelic order is eloquent of the order of the angelic cascade – but the mathematical numbers are themselves less important than the fact that they conform to an order as such. It is of no less theological importance that this ramifying order is, in the final analysis, beyond human comprehension.

Finicking over the celestial hierarchy may thus seem to court self-contradiction, when it is in fact working both sides of a paradox. We are urged to see that the universe is at once tuned to the nth degree, and by symmetries that are themselves theologically significant (notably, by 3s, 7s, and 9s), but also to recognise that it is ultimately beyond our ken. Similarly, when the size and shape of individual angels is glossed in categorical terms, the precise scale is not so germane as the idea – the divine reassurance and glory – of purposeful precision itself (see Figure 2).

**Figure 2** The Assumption of the Virgin by Francesco Botticini (1475–76), showing three hierarchies and nine orders of angels, each with different characteristics.

---

[48] English translation of this quotation by Rees (2013, 44).

Where angels are not anthropomorphic and size is specified, it is almost always to emphasise how large they are: in terms of travelling long distances, having one wing in the East and another in the West, filling the horizon, or stretching from the earth to the heavens. Such descriptions – which may tend to extraordinary specificity on, say, the distances between body parts – accent grandeur and importance (Burge 2012, 60–63). But on the rare occasions where angels are described as being notably tiny, that is also to press a symbolic significance. When hadith (§5) states that a 'single angel is smaller than a fly', the claim is part of an argument discussing how numerous angels are, as an expression of God's creative fecundity.[49] Still on the theme of flies, when Aquinas observed, 'We will never know the essence of a single fly'(Aquinas 2006, I-I, Q. 12, A. 5), he was making a broader claim about the limits of knowledge when it comes to essences, a limit that he says applies even to angels who can never fully know the essence of human beings either. God the creator alone can fully know His creation. As with attempts to specify the size of God, seen in, for instance, the *Shiūr Qomah* texts, the numbers are so vertiginously vast or miniscule that the purpose is to frustrate rather than enable conceptual completeness (Stroumsa 1983, 277).

Even the commonplace notion that angels have wings is a convenience for human comprehension rather than a corporeal fact. Aquinas says it snappily: 'Angels do not need bodies for their own sake but for ours' (Aquinas 2006, I-I, Q. 51, A. 2). Hildegard of Bingen emphasises that 'Angels do not have wings as birds do', but her comment appears in the context of what the conception of wings conjures for us, which is to suggest their inhuman speed but also their majesty (Hildegard of Bingen 1882, 75). That is why some Islamic angels are said to have wings of emerald (Rees 2013, 98). Hildegard denies the bird-wing image only to further stress this special capacity, claiming that they fly 'many times as fast as a bird, at the same pace that human thoughts travel' (Hildegard of Bingen 1882, 75).[50]

When we read about angels, then, and perhaps most vividly when we look at sculptures or paintings of them, their depictions do not presume verisimilitude to their form so much as they tell a story of what angels represent within their context. In a lost painting known only from Agostino Veneziano's engraving of 1516, Andrea del Sarto Pietà shows Christ flanked by three large angels, each discharging distinct duties of care, but our eyes are drawn most forcefully to the central angel whose wings do not here indicate the capacity for flight so much as for compassion, as they shield, with the angel's muscular arms,

---

[49] The innumerability of angels is made explicit by Pseudo-Dionysius: see Pseudo-Dionysius (1965, 60). See also Burge (2012, 60).

[50] See also Hildegard of Bingen (1882, 24), where the bird-wing image is denied in favour of their being 'still hovering flames in the power of God'.

Christ's shattered body. The wings also optically frame the scene, their tips rising above the hill of Golgotha to form an inverse triangle of the pyramidal form of the lower half of the picture that, as Meredith J. Gill has described it, positions the apex of each triangle as it meets Christ's foreshortened and upturned face on which this angel solemnly gazes (Gill 2014, 163). The picture is visually stunning but also theologically substantial, charged with the redemptive promise of Christ's overcoming death, enabled through his angels (see Figure 3).

The language of angelology in visual art thus tessellates with the ciphers of mathematics, because numbers too are deployed in a way that is essentially symbolic, to accent this or that feature. But numerical calculation does extra work as well, for the very reason that its language is more typically associated

**Figure 3** Agostino Veneziano, Pietà (engraving), after Andrea del Sarto, Puccini Pietà [1516].

with signs than symbols. Arithmetic within angelology reminds us of how Supermundane Intelligences, as Pseudo-Dionysius called the angels, surpass 'the feeble and limited range of our material numbers' (Pseudo-Dionysius 1965, 60).[51] Humans cannot compute them. More than this, the human system of numbering itself is inadequate. There is a lesson here about the limit of what it is possible to know about angels, but nested within that lesson, which manages expectations, is another that seeks to manage human pride and presumption.

Alexander Pope's *An Essay on Man: Epistle II* (1733) opens by re-working the wisdom of the Delphic oracle: 'Know then thyself, presume not God to scan; / The proper study of mankind is man' (Pope 2006, 281). This ethic of non-presumption has already been primed in the first Epistle, via the warning to 'Man', who is 'little less than Angel', but 'would be more': 'The bliss of man (could pride that blessing find) / Is not to act or think beyond mankind' (Pope 2006, 277). The warning is clear. Humans should not yearn for knowledge beyond their ordained state within the hierarchy of being, so that, returning to flies one final time, we ought not only to recognise but to be thankful for the fact that even the humble fly has capacities beyond us. 'Why has not Man a microscopic eye?', he asks: 'For this plain reason, Man is not a Fly' (Pope 2006, 277). The same ethic applies for our other senses too:

> Say what the use, were finer optics giv'n,
> T' inspect a mite, not comprehend the heav'n?
> Or touch, if tremblingly alive all o'er,
> To smart and agonize at ev'ry pore?
> Or quick effluvia darting thro' the brain,
> Die of a rose in aromatic pain?
> If nature thunder'd in his op'ning ears,
> And stunn'd him with the music of the spheres,
> How would he wish that Heav'n had left him still
> The whisp'ring Zephyr, and the purling rill? (Pope 2006, 277)

It is a highly seductive kind of hubris that Pope is describing here, an overreaching desire where the desire itself may be good and only the overreach proves fatal. What an exquisitely expressive image that is, to 'Die of a rose in aromatic pain'. The whole passage recalls the fate of the fallen angels as it has been rationalised, especially in the Christian tradition, from Aquinas's *Summa Theologiae* to Milton's *Paradise Lost* (Aquinas 2006, I-I, Q. 63, A. 2). What Pope tucks away in parenthesis, '(could pride that blessing find)', is the key to the puzzle. For it is pride, which leads to envy, and the lust for knowledge and therefore power beyond their station, that makes 'bliss' in God's love impossible. Pride is what caused the fall of Satan and his conspiring angels and led also to the

---

[51] Compare with the discussion of 'Feeble reason' in Section 1.

fall of man who plucked from the tree of knowledge. Milton has the Archangel Raphael join up these dots for Adam, advising humility to recognise that heaven is 'too high' for him 'To know what passes there', so that he should be 'lowly wise':

> Think only what concerns thee and thy being;
> Dream not of other worlds, what creatures there
> Live, in what state, condition or degree [. . .]. (Milton 2000, VIII: l. 172–176)

As for Satan, so for man: these plangent lines are an admonition against the very idea of angelology – straining to know what creatures angels might be, their state, condition, or degree. Aquinas surmises that Satan, ranked in the highest order of the angels, was surely of the class of Cherubim rather than Seraphim or Thrones, and fell into league with Powers and Principalities, because it is the Cherubim who are associated with 'knowledge and power' and therefore at risk of pride and envy. The Seraphim and Thrones, associated with the ardour of charity and the presence of God, are not by their natures liable to mortal sin in this way (Aquinas 2006, I-I, Q. 63, A. 2). Islamic accounts of pride and its dangers as the governing sin of sins is inflected through its angelology in a remarkably similar way, in the Qur'an's account of Iblīs, Satan's counterpart in Islam, who, as noted above, refused to bow down to Adam.[52]

Angelology as a discipline is in these several ways up against defined limits, and moral pitfalls too. The enterprise is made even more unstable by the fact that several influential angelologists speak of their subject as a highly rational form of scientific inquiry, while confessing to have come by their knowledge of angels from their own direct encounters with them, or with God. There is even at times a sense that the conditions for revelation may be compromised by the educated rationality associated with the scholar. Visionaries draw from a different well.

William Blake continued his communion with angels throughout his life, and a mystic such as Hildegard of Bingen drew on transcendent experiences and visions that actually grew more intense as she grew older. The more common trend, however, is that described by the likes of Thomas Traherne, who speaks of his childhood as a time of enchantment and adulthood as a time when he lost the capacity to access angelic 'intuition', and had to revert instead to 'reason', the latter offering only a shadow of what had once been revealed to him during his first 'Estate of Innocence'.[53] That revelation outdoes reason is not news, but

---

[52] For a discussion of this passage, including the question of whether Iblīs is an angel or in fact one of the unseen spirits, the jinn, see Murata (1987).

[53] Traherne (1908, 157). See Rees (2013, 49).

it has special implications for angelology. Whereas human knowledge may come through reason as much as intuition, angels are themselves said to learn exclusively from intuition according to Aquinas. The presumed authority of that other giant of the Christian tradition, Pseudo-Dionysius, was not derived from his powers as a scholar but from the mistaken belief that he had special authority of revelation as the Athenian convert of Paul the Apostle.

In practice, angelologists frequently tap a broad set of sources that include accounts of direct revelation and thoroughgoing scholarship, and a broad set of religious traditions too. Aquinas studied the Church Fathers who had come before him, but also Aristotelian science, Neoplatonic writings (notably, Proclus's *Elements of Theology* and the *Liber de causis*, an Arabic monotheistic reworking of the same text), Avicenna, and Maimonides. Availing of diverse texts, including religious writings and traditions outside of or opposed to the religion in question, is the rule rather than the exception. Yet angelology is characterised also by the contradistinctive ambition to refine, correct, and expose error. It is the perpetual challenge of the discipline to reconcile this tension.

Angelology in that respect offers a way of exploring continuities between the Abrahamic faiths. It may even provide a path into what Matthew Fox has called 'deep ecumenism', extending beyond the major monotheisms into the 'mystical traditions' of all the world religions, historical and contemporary (Fox and Sheldrake 1996, 25). There are accounts of angels that take this very capacious view, identifying continuities with the religious traditions that extend as far as the Sumerians and Akkadians, the Assyrians and Babylonians, the Persians, Egyptians and Greeks, as well as yet farther afield, to the Hindu Vedas (where angels appear as Gandharvas), and even to messenger spirits of shamanism found amongst the ancient Altaic tribes of Asia and the indigenous people of the Americas (Rees 2013, 1–2). That said, for all the ways angelology gestures towards a universalist impulse, the most substantial and influential interventions have been articulated within religious traditions that presuppose the exclusivity of the truth to which they bear witness. In practice, this has meant that the development of monotheistic religions has required theologians to rule out competing claims from other religions, unless it is able to absorb or assimilate them within a new logic.

Early Islamic scholars attempted the latter, for instance, when it came to Hellenic philosophy, and this led to some opportunistic relabelling of 'gods' as 'angels'. The substitutive move is telling, though not as straightforward as it sounds. For a start, although ancient Greek philosophy unfolded within a society that embraced polytheism, the greatest figures of antique thought, Plato and Aristotle, both recognised a plurality of divinities, while also acknowledging one divinity supreme above the others (Adamson 2016, 298):

> Thus in Plato's *Timaeus* a cosmic Demiurge is set over the so-called 'younger' gods as their father (40e–41a), and Aristotle famously compares the role of his unmoved mover to that of a king who presides over lesser celestial intellects (*Metaphysics*, 1076a, quoting the *Iliad*: 'the rule of many is not good; let there be one ruler'). Plotinus and other Neoplatonists likewise recognize divinities inferior to their completely unified first principle – even the heavenly bodies are called 'gods'. (*theoi*, at e.g. *Enneads*, 4.3.11)

This qualification is well taken, but the general point stands: readers of Greco-Arabic translations would have been misled by their translations, which sometimes simply eliminate references to 'gods', replacing them with 'angels', or else gloss over and eliminate pagan material (Adamson 2016, 299).[54] Adamson presses the fact that the main task facing Muslim authorities of Hellenic philosophy was usually not to explain away polytheistic tendencies in these texts, but rather to show that the First Principle or highest God of these texts could be identified with the God of Islam. Nonetheless, the will to reconcile religious traditions – the universalist impulse – leads to a situation in which angels entrench differences as well as continuities, differences that may themselves be dubious.

Returning, for instance, to the Qur'an's account of Iblīs refusing to bow down to Adam: that suggestive episode has been adduced by some Islamic scholars to contrast with the Christian view of angels, suggested in Pslam 8:5, that human beings were made of 'lower' status than angels.[55] But this verse is not dispositive; biblical accounts signal in other directions too, such as when John is told by an angel that he should not fall down in awe before him, because he is just another 'fellow servant' of God (Revelation 19:10). Paul puts humans above angels, reminding the Corinthians that 'we are to judge angels' (Corinthians 6:3). John Scottus Eriugena (ca.800-ca.877) is one of many in the subsequent Christian tradition to press this case for humans as in an important sense higher than angels; by his rationale, because human nature is uniquely made in the image and likeness of God (*Periphyseon*, IV.754a–b).

---

[54] 'For instance a section of Plotinus's *Enneads* on this topic (6.7.6–7) seems to have been purposefully eliminated in the Arabic version known as the *Theology of Aristotle* (Adamson 2002, 14). This same text is one of many that replace references to the One or First Principle with allusions to the "Creator", something that even happens in the Arabic version of Galen's paraphrase of the *Timaeus*' (Adamson 2016, 299). While Adamson's observations hold true for translations of Plotinus, made mainly in the ninth century, translations of Aristotle seem to have been undertaken more literally.

[55] On Jewish and Christian traditions parallel to the Qur'anic texts connected to the angels bowing down before Adam, see Zwemer (1937), where the emphasis is on tracing the origins of the Muslim version. See also Chipman (2002), who cites this source.

Disputations about angels may also arise within the same religion on the very same issues that supposedly define differences with other religions. The Egyptian-Ottoman scholar and theologian, Al-Bājūrī (1783–1860), diverges from Al-Laqānī and other Ash'arites on the matter of the superiority of angels to humans. While Al-Laqānī held that angels are superior to all humans other than the prophets, 'al-Bājūrī and al-Ṣāwī adopt the Māturīdī opinion that some non-prophets are better than some angels, as in the case of Abū Bakr, 'Umar, 'Uthman, and 'Alī who are deemed superior to the generality of angels other than Gabriel, Isrāfil, Mikā'īl, and 'Izrā'īl' (Spevack 2018, 544).[56]

Determining the precise status of angels within the hierarchy of being is in obvious ways a central consideration within any religion seeking to reconcile the idea of a Supreme Being. The balance is delicate. Angels invite veneration, but not angelolatry. While the Abrahamic faiths suggest it is appropriate to recognise Satan and his demon underlings as real beings, the idea of interfering fallen angels may encourage a vision of the world as a battleground between two equal forces, Good and Evil. 'Some religions have seen the world in these terms, but that is not monotheism': Roger Trigg makes the point that a Supreme Being can hardly be 'Supreme' if He and the world He created is vulnerable to a spiritual adversary.[57]

Given these inter- and infra-religious challenges, it is easy to see why angelology should shrink before the stringencies of contemporary scholarship. Maximally open and creatively syncretic but also fiercely partisan and exclusive, the dialectic is dizzying. Worse: it is a patchy, provisional, and faith-dependent mode of inquiry that often trades in scientific language, but in a way that should mostly be interpreted symbolically. Veering from the efforts of 'highest reason' to Scriptural and private revelation makes angelology vulnerable on several fronts at the same time, all the more so when integrated, as it aims to be, within broader philosophical and theological traditions. The discipline slips and slides between domains of knowledge to the extent that it feels reminiscent of the pre-professional academy, before the sciences and the arts, never mind religion, had been formally disaggregated. Is angelology after all a hopelessly unreconstructed enterprise? A closer look at the early modern period, at the cusp of when the professionalised academy began to take its current shape, provokes the opposite possibility. It may instead be the modern academy that is inadequate and needs re-constructing.[58]

Dr John Dee, celebrated scientist but also sometime occultist, was mentioned briefly already. He is useful to recall here for the way he would confidently draw

---

[56] See also Spevack (2014, 27).    [57] See Trigg (2020, 17–18).
[58] On the limitations and hubris of contemporary scientific thought, how 'Dogmatic ideology, fear-based conformity and institutional inertia are inhibiting scientific creativity', see Sheldrake (2013, 4; passim).

a distinction between his conversations with angels and his dabbling with magical practices.[59] From a contemporary perspective, his angelology is indistinguishable from magic; seems indistinguishable indeed from his most important source on the subject, Pseudo-Dionysius (who had such a vast influence on Christian thinkers at large within the early modern period).[60] Dee's speculative mode appears very much the same in all of the domains that piqued his interest. Like his work on alchemy, his enthusiasm for angels was conceived as part of an experimental scientific enterprise. The records of his conversations with angels make vivid his instrumental purpose (Harkness 1999b, 9–59). He had reached the end of the road as far as contemporary scholarship would take him – from mathematics, to astrology, to optics, to geography, to navigation, to history – and so he sought wisdom on the Book of Nature from the very author of that book. Or as close as he could get, through His emissaries. Angelology was an attempt to establish a unified and coherent basis for all religious belief alongside rather than against science (Harkness 1999a, 130). Knowledge of angels helped him to better understand the world scientifically, and his understanding of the structures and workings of the world was the spur for his convictions about the divine order of which angels were a part (see Figure 4).[61]

Dee's angelology was breathtakingly broad, 'a synthesis of lore about angels drawn from Islamic, Jewish, and Christian authors', suggestive of the cross-fertilisation of theology within the Abrahamic traditions on angels, and of something more surprising too. His eclectic openness when it came to angels reflected and encouraged that same mode in his scientific inquiry (Harkness 1999a, 110). Dee's life-example is in that respect fascinatingly generalisable. Trace the development of angelology against the historical development of human inquiry and the study of angels neither contradicts nor compromises the *thymos* of science, which was actually – here is the great untold story of angelology – born from the same impulse. Dial back the clock yet further, and this potentially scandalous truth comes into sharper focus.

While 1543 is often given as the ground zero for science as we know it today (Dee conducted his conversations with angels between 1583 and 1587), there are good reasons to regard modern science as beginning much earlier, within an even more open atmosphere of inquiry at ease with, and indeed nurtured by, the sovereignty of divine power. The decisive theological nudge has even been

---

[59] See Harkness (1999a, 98); also: 'Dee and his contemporaries drew fine – sometimes very fine – distinctions between magic, religion, and natural philosophy [. . .] Often, authors of the period made a particular point of excepting communication with angels from other forms of magic' (Harkness 1999a, 123). See also Walker (1975).

[60] For Dionysius's influence on cosmology and theology, see Knowles (1975, 79–94, passim).

[61] See French (1972) and Clulee (1988).

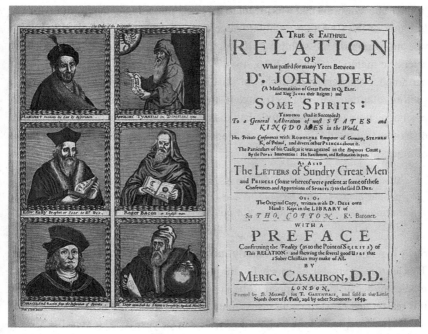

**Figure 4** Florence Estienne Méric Casaubon (1599–1671), A True and Faithful Relation of what Passed for Many Yeers between Dr. John Dee [ . . . ] and Some Spirits, London, 1659.

associated with a single year, when the 1277 Condemnations affirmed God's absolute power. In a stroke, Nicholas Spencer contends, it was possible to question everything previously assumed about the world and how it works, including the previously inviolable authority of Aristotle (Spencer 2023, 78–83).

One set of dogmas did not thereby replace another; rather, 1277 opened a new vista for hypothetical constructs, which multiplied under the rubric of *secundum imaginationem* ('according to the imagination'). Angelology thrived under these conditions. 'Could one angel be in two places at the same time? Could two occupy the same space simultaneously? Did angels move between different spaces with finite or instantaneous speed' (Spencer 2023, 82)? However far removed from scientific inquiry such questions might seem, the intellectual conditions that made them possible were essential to the development of science as we know it. For these questions about angels were of a piece, and often themselves in the furtherance of inquiry liberated by the warrant to think with unprecedented audacity.

Discussing the nature and function of angels catalysed 'strange new thought worlds' (Spencer 2023, 83). Thirteenth-century scholastic theologians elaborated 'a scientific synthesis that was meant to express optimally the intelligibility of the teaching of the Christian tradition concerning angels and demons', but the aim was not primarily to establish a theological synthesis 'according to a specially scientific method' (Bonino 2016, 46, 47).[62] The aim was highly practical, as it pertained to the perfection of the spiritual life. Angelology provided the tools for such revolutionary thinking. To take just one example, it was newly possible to posit a vacuum (an idea Aristotle had dismissed), and from that followed further questions that would invite generative answers, and themselves prove generative of other questions:

> Would a stone placed in this void be capable of rectilinear motion? Would people in a vacuum be able to see or hear one another? Why wouldn't surrounding celestial spheres not collapse in through the void? (Spencer 2023, 82)

Such hypotheticals have 'a peculiarly modern feel to them' (Spencer 2023, 82). This is true every bit as much for the questions that superficially sound most medieval, because they happen to be couched with reference to angels. It is for this reason that Edward Grant insists that, 'if we must assign a date for the birth of modern science, we would, without doubt, choose the year 1277' (Grant 1962, 200).

An important caveat is overdue here. Spencer, Grant, and other scholars who press the paradigm-shifting significance of the 1277 Condemnations take their cue from Pierre Duhem's revisionary history of classical and medieval science. That work is more than a century old now, and looks somewhat naïve and reductive in the light of historical materials that have subsequently come to light. In the Latin West, it was after all around twenty years earlier that people had gained a full understanding of Aristotelian science, and this science was generally accepted in its main features until the late seventeenth century. Thought experiments are also a feature of philosophy long before 1277 (for instance, Boethius's *per impossibile* conjecture in *Opuscula Sacra* 3 about the Good if God did not exist). It may be, then, that the Condemnations were not decisively causative of this shift in speculative thought after all, that it was instead part of a longer-term intellectual development incipient before the Condemnations, and which also continued to unfold for some time afterwards.[63] Still, there remains firm agreement on the shift itself, and on its consequences being momentous. That is the essential headline. For all the recent scholarly refinements and riders, there remains a pressing truth within the now mainly discarded Duhemian thesis that 'the late thirteenth century brought a dramatic step, onto a new path, in medieval thought'; and that,

---

[62] In support of his observation, Bonino cites Maritain (1995).
[63] For an authoritative overview, see Emery and Speer (2001).

moreover, 'this step, confident, innovative and self-consciously critical of Aristotle, would lead along a course continuing over the next two centuries and carrying on, at ever-increasingly velocity, into the modern world' (Marrone 2001, 297–98).

Rethinking the relationship between natural science and the science of angelology enriches our understanding of both.[64] The influence was mutual, as the study of each also yields independent value. While advocating for the historical and persistent value of angelology as a stalking horse for other kinds of intellectual inquiry – including, and even especially, philosophy and science – it is important not to lose sight of its immense value on its own terms, for understanding the nature of God and religious belief. The final section of this Element turns to why angels are so consequential for theology, and for monotheism in particular.

## 4 Angels within Monotheism

Angels have played a decisive role in all major religious traditions, from the *yazatas* of Zoroastrianism, the *'utras* of Mandean religion, and the *daimons* of Platonism, to the Abrahamic religions of Christianity, Judaism, and Islam, to the Indian religions of Hinduism, Buddhism, Sikhism, to the New Age recovery of pre-Christian Celtic, Gnostic, and Pagan supernatural intercessors. For all that, monotheistic religions are also a special case. For in contrast to the ancient polytheisms that gathered their beliefs and practices through custom, tradition and oral testimony, 'the monotheistic religion was *written* in a book whose *author* is *God*' (Bettini 2014, 108). Religions of the book cannot drift as other religions do, insofar as they are accountable to their foundational document. The distinction is broadly analogous to the way the American Constitution was designed to anchor the law of the United States of America, as against the common law practice of the United Kingdom, which is more deliberately self-developing, through legal precedent.

The analogy is suggestive but limited. There is an essential difference between the authoritative status of foundational legal texts and the Scriptures of monotheism. Any text may be misinterpreted or interpreted in bad faith; as it may likewise be interpreted by different governing principles: 'originalist' versus 'living', say, when it comes to the American Constitution; or within religion, fundamentalist versus progressive. Yet the status of the monotheistic Scriptures is *sui generis*. It is different not only from legal or political documents but also from other documents of religious history and theology, such as Hesiod's *Theogony*, or

---

[64] On how, *contra* Duhem, the 'scientific' notions of fourteenth-century thinkers are incommensurate with the approach of modern science, see Murdoch (1991).

Varro's *Antiquities of Human and Divine Things*. The plain reason is that the Scriptures of the monotheistic religions bear a divine imprimatur.[65] Words written by human beings, even words about God, cannot compete with the authority of words believed to be *of* God.

Angelology never could therefore have been an optional feature of monotheism: the importance of angels cannot be gainsaid in a context that takes such claims to be divinely revealed. 'Agreement among theologians about the specifics of angelic nature was not possible given the transcendence of the objects of speculation, but angels figure so large in scripture and devotion that the subject could not be avoided' (Peers 2001, 2).

There is another, complementary reason why, for religions of the book, the study of angels could not – and still cannot – be avoided; simply, because they are necessary for understanding those same foundational books. This is obviously true when it comes to an angel of the high status of Gabriel, who intervenes at defining moments of all the Abrahamic faiths, as recorded in each of their foundational books, and in extra-canonical texts too, such as the Book of Enoch, the rabbinical commentaries, and the Kabbalah. The role Gabriel plays is of a supporter and messenger whose status secures the truth and authority of his activities.[66] To misunderstand his status is to misunderstand the events in which he appears.[67] The same practice of interpreting Scripture through angels applies to more subtle references as well, when individual angels are not important enough to be named, or when referred to as a group. It is an ongoing exegetical process.

The discovery of the Qumrân texts as late as 1956, for instance, has shed light on the meaning of Paul's injunction for women to keep their heads covered in church, following the enigmatic rationale that they should do so, in part, 'on account of the angels': διὰ τοὺς ἀγγέλους (I Corinthians xi. 10). The phrase has been the subject of lively debate since Tertullian, and while this new evidence about angels does not definitively end that debate, it does more than add another interpretation to many: it shores up an already existing view, rendering others less probable (Fitzmyer 1957).

The study of Scripture informs the study of angels, then, but the study of angels also informs the study of Scripture – and not only Scripture, the complete religious

---

[65] For a discussion in this vein, see Bettini (2014, 108).

[66] In Judaism, Gabriel features as a helper to Daniel and a warrior for God's causes, and he is the only angel actually named in the Hebrew Bible; in Christianity, he announces John the Baptist's birth to his father, Zacharias, and reveals to the Virgin Mary that she will conceive a son by the power of the Holy Spirit; in Islam, as Jibra'il, he dictates Allah's words to the Prophet Muhammad on the Night of Power (Laylat al-Qadr), the very text of the Qur'an.

[67] Gabriel plays a prominent role in all the Abrahamic faiths, but his status varies: in Judaism, he may be ranked alongside Michael, and to some extent in Christianity too; in Islam, he is the most important of all the angels, such that his role is unique.

cosmology, which includes human beings and God Himself.[68] This feedback loop has been broken by modern angelology, which neglects or denies the status of angels as divinely created beings within a divine order. In Judaism, angels are described as such throughout the Tanakh, rabbinic literature, apocrypha and pseudepigrapha, and traditional liturgy. Christianity takes up and elaborates this assumption within the Bible (which contains 273 references to angels), and its articles of faith and its traditions, notably through the person of Christ. Islam makes angels a fundamental part of its religious belief (mentioned 78 times in the Qur'an), as it pertains to everything from eschatology to law and theology to devotional practices, such that their rejection constitutes *kufr* (unbelief).[69]

When the Abrahamic faiths seek to explain away angels, they come up against a further theological obstacle expressive of their primary definition. For the very name 'angel' refers not to what it is – its size or shape or capacities – but to what it does. The English word derives from the Greek ἄγγελος *(angelos)*, and the earlier Hebrew מַלְאָךְ *(mal'āk)*, both of which imply an emissary; and there is also a suggestive lexical connection with an Arabic verb 'to send'.[70] Angels are defined by their activity, not only as emissaries but in other highly specialised roles too. To treat them as if they are vestigial cultural encumbrances that might be shed is therefore to underestimate the centrality of their role as agents who continuously shape the way things work. 'The entire corporeal world is governed by God through his angels', Aquinas thought (Aquinas 2006, I-I, Q. 63, A. 7). He goes further, speaking in a philosophical grammar that turns them from nouns into verbs. They are the expression of their actions *(operatio)*: 'an angel is in a place by acting there' (Aquinas 2006, I-I, Q. 52, A. 2). Far from being dispensable ornaments within the celestial realm, they are integral to that realm, and to our world too, in which they are sustained and known and existent at all by virtue of their doing.

Given all this, it is worth returning once more to the question of why the status of angels has been so degraded by modern theologians. To the several reasons already given must be added one more that lies buried within the subtext of modern scholarship, and only occasionally peeps out. Angels have been historicised out of existence in part because they have proved incompatible

---

[68] On how Scriptural exegesis led to an expansion of the knowledge of and interest in angels across the Abrahamic faiths, see Olyan (1993), Burge (2012, 32–33), Gallorini (2021).

[69] This point is well noted at the opening of Burge (2012, 3), with supporting credal statements. See also Watt (1994, 41, 43, 52–54, 62, 72, 83).

[70] Brown, Driver, and Briggs (2000, 521). On the defining role of angels as messengers, see Rees (2013, 1–18; 95–104). The Arabic lexical link is suggestive but should not be overstated, given that the connection of the noun *(malak)* to the verbal form is comparatively tenuous and the verbal form does not seem to have been used in Arabic other than in discussions of what the word means.

with the dominant contemporary view of religion as subject to a progressive, evolutionary development. By this principle, as different religions can be said to be more and less evolved, so too individual religions evolve. In broad strokes, 'evolution' here is understood as a kind of growing up, a leaving behind of childish things; it means abandoning naïve literalism in favour of symbolic sophistication. Belief systems are implicitly ranked according to their epistemological respectability on this scale.

At the lowest rung, there is pre-scientific ignorance, to be bracketed off as superstition and magic. Hence why the animisms and polytheisms of ancient Greece and Rome are pejoratively described as pagan or idolatrous, and mostly not glossed as religions at all, but as myths.[71] Then there is a middle category, for religions that present like those of the medieval and early modern period: presuming a spiritual world to be operative within the physical, but in a way that is increasingly accountable to modern science. The supernatural plays a lively part, but those still intoxicated by the numinous are sobering to the good sense of empiricism; prayer is also overtaking the instrumental incantations of occultism.[72] The highest rung, the most respectable of all, is reserved for religions that have purified themselves into deism, where the self is 'buffered' to the extent of extinguishing the possibility of experiencing the spiritual altogether.[73]

The bias of such taxonomies is not as acute as it was a few decades ago. Robert Orsi strikes an optimistic note in his account of how it is possible to operate between belief and analysis, faith and scholarship. 'No one any longer holds the secularization thesis to be universally true', he observes: 'Scholars no longer have to present the powerful religious idioms of the modern world as atavistic holdovers of a vanishing time or as distorted reactions against modernity' (Orsi 2004, 10, 12). That is salutary, but towards the end of the same study, he concedes that scholars nonetheless remain under pressure to interpret religion by a logic that insinuates several intertwined prejudices: not only scientistic and secular, but also presentist (progress is always improvement, and newest is best), and ethno-imperialistic (religions brought by colonialism are superior to indigenous beliefs and practices):[74]

> True religion, then, is epistemologically and ethically singular. It is rational, respectful of persons, noncoercive, mature, nonanthropomorphic in its higher

---

[71] See Bettini (2014).

[72] The historical record suggests that religion and magic were tightly tangled imaginaries, rather than belief systems that ran in parallel, or in which religion rose while magic fell in popularity, practice, and respectability: See Valerie I. J. Flint on how the invocation of angels became interwoven in the early medieval Christian Church with magical practices that were on the rise in the same period (Flint 1991, especially 157–72). See also Keck (1998, 173–74).

[73] See Taylor (2007, 539) discussed in Section 2.

[74] See Burge (2012, 10).

forms, mystical (as opposed to ritualistic), unmediated and agreeable to democracy (no hierarchy in gilded robes and fancy hats), monotheistic (no angels, saints, demons, ancestors), emotionally controlled, a reality of mind and spirit not body and matter. It is concerned with ideal essences not actual things, and especially not about presences in things. (Orsi 2004, 188)

This list of markers collectively suggests what makes for a fully evolved religion; but the individual items are not equal. Some subsume others, and one above all defines the rest. Belief in a single deity is effectively what it means to be 'rational, respectful of persons, noncoercive, mature, nonanthropomorphic in its higher forms, mystical (as opposed to ritualistic)', as well as 'emotionally controlled, a reality of mind and spirit not body and matter', 'concerned with ideal essences not actual things, and especially not about presences in things'. To be monotheistic within modernity is to be all these things, the fullest expression of which involves the final step on from orthodox Judaism, Christianity, and Islam, which is to trivialise, and so marginalise, 'angels, saints, demons, ancestors'. This step is inevitable because it represents – so the argument goes – the spiritual equivalent of the earthly impulse towards political and social systems of culture and government that are 'unmediated and agreeable to democracy'. By the postmodern redux logic of hard-line Protestantism, 'no hierarchy in gilded robes and fancy hats' means, *a fortiori*, 'no angels, saints, demons, ancestors'.[75]

Where monotheism is the most 'evolved' of religious types, the most evolved form of monotheism – fully weaned from pre-modern ignorance in favour of liberal-democratic, scientific-materialist enlightenment – requires the death of God. Shy of that, insofar as monotheisms wish still to avow theistic belief, there is deism, in which religion is denuded to *deus otiosus*, the belief in a creator God who has entirely withdrawn from what He has created. Angels have no standing in this cosmology. As the indirect hand of God, they must be explained away. That means relegating them to history (they were once active but are no longer), or by a more thoroughgoing rationalisation, the records of angelic intervention are re-interpreted to suggest they were never really real in the first place.

As noted in Section 1, Bettini exemplifies this constructivist view, which he takes to its fullest conclusion by questioning whether monotheism is even possible. What presents as such is, he contends, 'nothing more than a polytheism in disguise' (Bettini 2014, 67). Of the Abrahamic faiths, Christianity is *prima facie* the most vulnerable to this charge, given its panoply of elevated figures that include 'angels, saints, demons', but also the Virgin Mary and the

---

[75] On the arresting connection between scientific materialism and postmodernism, see Iain McGilchrist on their 'left-hemisphere' thinking: 'They share a sense of superiority, born of the conviction that others are taken in by illusions, to which those in the know have the explanation' (McGilchrist 2010, 426).

doctrine of the Trinity, which Henry Corbin is quick to remind us was, for the Greek Fathers of the Church, 'égale distance du monothéisme et du polythéisme' (Corbin 1981b, 13). This charge must be met head on, not least for the ways in which angelologists themselves seem to court it. No lesser a figure than Pseudo-Dionysius writes of how 'the Word of God not only calls these celestial beings above us gods, but also gives this same name to saintly men amongst us, and to those men who, in the highest degree, are lovers of God'. (Pseudo-Dionysius 1965, Ch XII, 53–53). Importantly, this passage quoted from Pseudo-Dionysius comes with a careful qualification. Apotheosis is nested within monotheism:

> [. . .] although the first and unmanifest God superessentially transcends all things, being enthroned above all, and therefore none of the beings or things which are can truly be said to be like him, save in so far as those intellectual and rational beings who are wholly turned towards union with him, as far as possible, to the divine radiance, in the imitation of God (if it be lawful so to speak) with all their powers, are thought worthy of the same divine name. (Pseudo-Dionysius 1965, XII, 53–53)

God continues to reign Supreme within this scheme, but the idea of celestial beings as gods nonetheless invites the possibility that Abrahamic angels might all be related, and moreover related to the *devas* of Hinduism, and to the gods of many other religions too. Dionysius himself does after all explicitly recognise the protecting gods of Egypt and Babylon as angelic (Pseudo-Dionysius 1965, Ch. XI, 46–49). Concede this, and monotheism begins to look very much as Bettini would have it: a merely rhetorical re-composting of the belief in multiple deities. There is, even so, a third way of reading the evidence.

Bettini has an atheistic drum to bang, and his contention that monotheism is polytheism in disguise flows from his conviction that all religions are disguised psychology. But retreating from the idea that monotheism and polytheism are neat antinomies does not imply that they are neatly identical. The historical development of angelology tells a messier story in which monotheism does not define itself in flat contradistinction to polytheism, but instead seeks to understand spiritual beings within a hierarchy. Rupert Sheldrake puts it this way:

> The gods in polytheistic religions are assimilated into monotheism by being treated as angels. If the many gods are recognised as subject to the supreme God, they can be accepted as divine intermediaries and as divine powers. The difference between monotheism and polytheism, as first sight so stark, is softened and modified by the recognition of angels. (Fox and Sheldrake 1996, 66–67)

It is important to tread carefully here. So much depends on what, exactly, is meant by 'gods' being 'treated as angels'. 'Assimilated' could mean several things, including a theological sleight of hand. Monotheism did not appear out of thin air; it emerged from a cultural context dominated by polytheism, and it took centuries to fully establish itself. There was no clean break, even for Islam. Pre-Islamic Meccan deities were occasionally labelled 'angels' to diminish their status versus God. Angels were deployed in anti-polytheistic polemics against Meccan polytheists, but also against *other* monotheisms:[76] 'Far from representing a denigration of an absolute divine singularity [. . .] angelology and demonology could sometimes accompany the elevation of one deity and the resultant reconfiguration of the structure and contours of divine multiplicity' (Reed 2020, 53).

Until quite recently within religious studies, 'monotheism was widely celebrated as the invention of ancient Israel and its unique contribution to the progress of human civilization' (Schäfer 2018, 1). Partly as a result, the increased interest in angels and demons in post-exilic Jewish literature was interpreted as 'a phenomenon of decline or devolution, and it remains common to explain this development in terms of the trauma of the Babylonian Exile and/ or blame it on the corrupting influence of the polytheism of the foreign empires that thereafter ruled the Land of Israel' (Reed 2020, 49).[77] It is reasonable to speculate as to why references to angels and demons are comparatively rare and vague in the Hebrew Bible – with only passing, unnamed allusions to 'hosts' and 'holy ones' and mysterious messengers – but then suddenly multiply and crystallise between the Babylonian exile (586–38 BC) and the compilation of the Mishnah (ca. 200 AD).[78] As already noted in Section 1, however, the need for angels at times of crisis does not prove that they are simply fantasised into existence. If they do indeed exist, such times may reasonably be when they are enjoined to be most active, and human beings most attuned to them. It is peremptory to assume that the change represents, as Christian scholars have often contended, 'a religious environment in which the strict monotheism of the Old Testament prophets (and Jesus himself) had been significantly weakened' (Stuckenbruck and North 2004, 6). It may seem like common sense to read the Second Temple interest in angels as 'compensatory for Jewish feelings of "distance" from God after the Exile', but this view is driven by the contestable, supersessionist assumption that the rise of interest in angels was just one stage on the road towards full religious development; specifically, an intertestamental trajectory from the Hebrew Bible to the New Testament (Reed 2020, 7).

---

[76] See Hawting (1999, 144–49). For a discussion of this claim, see Burge (2012, 11).

[77] On the numerous, including recent, attempts to explain the rise of interest in angels and demons within Second Temple Judaism as a result of the 'influence' of 'pagan' polytheism, Reed cites Tuschling (2007, 14–28). On the framing in terms of post-exilic trauma, see Reed (2020, Ch. 2).

[78] See Reed (2020, 5).

Prescinding the loaded logic of evolution versus devolution, then, speaking more neutrally of change (without prejudice as to whether positive or negative), it can be said that the major monotheisms harden their commitment to belief in a single deity over the centuries. To that straightforward observation must be added the more enigmatic fact that as monotheisms become, as it were, more monotheistic, they also become more invested in angels. An unexpected turn of events, given that other spiritual beings complicate and potentially compromise the status of a Supreme Being. But angelology already recognises and forestalls that jeopardy. The cosmic cautionary tale of the fall of the angels rings out. The first and defining feature of the celestial order is that God has no rival.

Recognising error does not, of course, itself prevent the possibility of falling into that same error. The early Christian Church struggled to stay on the right side of angelolatry: 'the New Testament testifies to a certain distrust' regarding the worship of angels, Bonino concedes, so much so that he repairs to the same language of 'disguise' found within Bettini's account. Except that when he asks, 'Does it not conceal a disguised polytheism?', his question is not rhetorical (Bonino 2016, 274). He opens up the contention that Bettini closes down, through his subsequent account of how the early Church sought 'to subordinate the angels to Christ', the acknowledged necessity of arriving at 'a clear qualitative distinction between the cult reserved for God and the one that can be rendered to the angels', and the careful distinctions made by Councils and many of the most influential figures of the Christian tradition between giving angels honour, which they deserve, without tipping into idolatry.[79]

History tells of these efforts to disambiguate the status of angels relative to God. That is the challenge of 'assimilation' to which Sheldrake refers, and it has been imperfectly achieved: 'the borderline between cultic acts reserved to God and those that result from simple veneration is sometimes uncertain' (Bonino 2016, 274, 275–76). There have surely been substantive differences on how to draw the line, such that a figure like Augustine thought building churches in honour of the angels was a blameworthy act, whereas major orders of the Catholic Church, notably the Benedictines and the Jesuits, went on to do just that, as well as enshrining devotion to angels in their readings and liturgies (Bonino 2016, 276–78).

Given the internal religious debates on how to engage angels, it is hardly surprising that monotheisms should also fight out this question between themselves. Whatever confidence is required for a given monotheism to define itself

---

[79]  See, for instance, the Council of Laodicea (343–81 AD), which specified that 'Christians must not forsake the Church of God, and go away and invoke angels'; anyone engaging in such 'forbidden', 'covert idolatry' shall be 'anathema': 'for he has forsaken our Lord Jesus Christ, the Son of God, and has gone over to idolatry'. Canon 35 (Percival (tr.) 1960, 151).

against polytheism, there is something especially charged about the way the Abrahamic faiths press their respective differences against each other, jostling within their shared religious inheritance. To Freud's language of the 'narcissism of small differences' might be added what Rabbi Johnathan Sacks dubbed the Abrahamic dynamics of 'sibling rivalry'.[80] Whatever the tendency towards exaggeration within such a context, not all credal differences between the Abrahamic faiths can be waved away as minor or inconsequential; some are clearly substantive and insuperable. The Qur'an could hardly be clearer in its conviction that Christian Trinitarianism is a fundamental violation of what it means to believe in a single deity, for instance, Islam affirming by contrast that God has no parts, is not incarnated, and has no progeny: 'Say, "Praise be to God, who has no child! He has no partner in sovereignty; nor has He any protector from meekness." And proclaim His Greatness!' (Q al-Isrā' 17:111).[81]

If there is indeed anything in the charge that Christianity is disguised polytheism, how far are Judaism and Islam vulnerable to the same imputation? Islam is from the start the most self-consciously and stridently monotheistic of the Abrahamic faiths, and yet it is no less, and in some ways more, theologically committed to the reality and importance of angels. It is a potent conundrum. 'The Qur'an emerged in contestation with a polytheistic culture, and affirming God's unity (*tawhīd*) is its most fundamental tenet', and yet angels are given a many-sided role in that same holy book (Haleem 2008, 26): to convey God's messages to the Prophets (32:51), to encourage and pray for the believers (40:7–9), to record human actions (50:17–18), to take human souls at death (32:11), to praise God (2:30), and to carry His throne (Haleem 2008, 27). The Qur'an was always going to be heavily engaged with angels, it might be answered, given that it was itself revealed by an angel. But such reasoning is unproductively circular – what then explains why the Qur'an was so revealed? – and cannot allay the suspicion that monotheistic religions have rebranded as angels the polytheistic gods they pretend to have abandoned.

Recent scholarship has tempered the assumption that the Abrahamic faiths assembled their angelologies by influencing each other. When it comes to their iconographic representation, early scholarship overstated the extent to which Jewish angelology was inflected by Zoroastrianism, and Islamic angelology by the Judeo-Christian tradition (Burge 2012, 32). Nonetheless, there are clear and obvious overlaps, when it comes to named angels, and in other, deeper philosophical respects too. Muslim philosophers informed by ancient Greek (especially Aristotelian) thought 'developed new branches of knowledge that

---

[80] Sacks uses the term some thirty-nine times in his explanatory account of the historical and current tensions between the Abrahamic faiths, in Sacks (2015).

[81] See Ibrahim (2022, 27).

combined angelology, cosmology, and epistemology, shaping Christian and Jewish philosophical and mystical trajectories' (Ahuvia 2021, 211–12).[82]

Claims of influence between these religions can also be controversial. It has been argued that the idea of a human figure bearing angelic or even divine status was inspired by an ancient Jewish tradition (Hurtado 2010, 560). That angel speculation generated Christology is very much a minority view, but it is suggestive of how the subject of angels can lead to potentially explosive conclusions. Surveying how the Abrahamic faiths have interacted, it is necessary to distinguish between *influenced by* and *derived from*. In the example just given: it can both be true that Jewish conceptions of angels informed the emergent Christian understanding of Christ, and also that 'the impetus of earliest Christological claims lies in the formative experiences of early believers, especially experiences which they understood as encounters with, and visions of, the risen and glorified Jesus' (Hurtado 2010, 560–61).[83]

By this textured approach, exploring the status and provenance of angels within a given monotheism invites comparison with other faith traditions, while avoiding reductive assumptions that confuse influence with derivation, and extrinsic with intrinsic features. The modern awkwardness about angels, though, inhibits this ecumenical impulse. They are more often avoided in discussion, for being theologically 'immature' encumbrances,[84] a bias in some cases so strong that scholars have not been content to consign angels to history: they have rewritten history itself, to suggest that angels were never really that important anyway. To take one telling example, Yehezkel Kaufmann's account of the origins of Judaism popularised in the modern Jewish mind the idea that exclusive monotheism was the singular triumph of ancient Israel (Kaufmann 1960, 63). Angels were pushed to the margins, where they had been central for most of Jewish history. The difference between Judaism and the other ancient polytheisms from which it sprang is thereby exaggerated. While Kaufmann's account has since been refuted by scholars, his view of angels as non-Jewish persists in many circles and has passed into the popular imagination through seminaries and rabbinical training (Ahuvia 2021, 215–16).

Angels have thus been doubly disavowed within modernity: historicised, to deny their objective existence (they come down to use as a cultural delusion), but also written out of history altogether (denying that any such delusions were

---

[82]  See also Davidson (1992).

[83]  On how 'The excessive reliance upon angels within Second Temple Judaism posed a threat to the pre-eminence of Christ among Jewish Christians of the first century', see Gleason (2003, 107).

[84]  This loaded term is used by Othmar Keel in surveying early Judaism that demanded allegiance to Yahweh alone, but in a way that implicitly recognised the existence of other gods: he calls that phrase 'immature monotheism': See Assmann (2007). Quoted by Bettini (2014, 35).

ever suffered). While it is beyond the limits of scholarship to take on the objective existence of angels, the historical record at least is indubitable. Whatever else might be claimed about angels, it is clear that they were leading protagonists in the development of the Abrahamic monotheisms, including the establishment of monotheism *as* monotheism. Jameson paints a vivid picture:

> Those nations who acknowledged one Almighty Creator, and repudiated with horror the idea of a plurality of Gods, were the most willing to accept, the most enthusiastic in accepting these objects of an intermediate homage, and gladly placed between their humanity and the awful supremacy of an unseen God, the ministering spirits who were the agents of his will, the witnesses of his glory, the partakers of his bliss, and who in their preternatural attributes of love and knowledge filled up that vast space in the created universe which intervened between mortal man, and the infinite, omnipotent LORD OF ALL. (Jameson 2012, I, 47)

None of which is to suggest that the relationship between God, gods, and angels was easily or harmoniously negotiated. In late antiquity, enough polytheists outside Christianity and Judaism evidently viewed angels as alternatives to their own local gods that the fear of idolatry was febrile – leading, ultimately, to the iconoclasm of the eighth and ninth centuries. The 'rejection of images of angels was directly related to that fear of idolatry, but it also involved other issues of primary concern in the early Church, namely the worship of angels as gods and pagan attempts to equate Christian angels with their own Gods' (Peers 2001, 15). Something of the same unfolded within Judaism too. The iconoclastic era left its mark on the archaeological record of the synagogues of Byzantine Palestine where Jews themselves likely carried out the disfiguring of images, targeting especially 'winged figures on synagogue lintels'. Once acceptable in synagogue art, after the iconoclastic era, the depiction of angels was limited to illuminated manuscripts (Ahuvia 2021, 208).[85]

The trouble angels pose to monotheism is even more fundamental than erupts with angelolatry. Whether or not they are worshipped, the existence of angels as such is a liability. While Aquinas amongst others emphasised the nature of angels as created beings, and so limited in their powers, Augustine would not have dedicated the space he did in the *City of God* to asking whether or not we ought to worship angels, and – having answered in the negative – what does in fact constitute properly ordered worship, if he did not think it was a live question.[86] Angelological ideas and practices unsettle first century Christian writers for the apparent conflict they present to Christ's soteriological and

---

[85] See also Hachlili (2013, 276).
[86] On Augustine's theology of worship with a focus on angels, see Wiebe (2021, 59–72).

cosmological pre-eminence, and the problem does not entirely go away in the ensuing centuries (Stuckenbruck and North 1995, 203). It persists because the question of how humans should regard angels is inherently difficult to answer. Augustine's intervention is correspondingly notable for the clean lines he draws, presenting worship of angels not as the mere excess of their quite proper veneration, but as a perfect perversion, an expressly demonic enterprise:

> Unlike the demons, who seek happiness by drawing praise to themselves, the good angels seek at all times to turn us to the true source of happiness, God, who has also made them happy. If the marked characteristic of the demons was their unrelenting pursuit of praise for themselves, then the life of the good angels is exactly the opposite: holy angels refuse to be worshiped themselves 'for they do not wish us to worship them as our gods, but to join them in worshipping their God and ours; not to sacrifice to them, but together with them to become a sacrifice to God'. (Wiebe 2021, 61)[87]

That good angels 'refused to be worshipped' looks to solve the problem, though it actually only displaces the responsibility from the would-be worshipper onto the angels; but angels were never the problem. Human beings remain primed to commit the same blasphemy. Polytheistic religions clearly do not face this same difficulty, because angels may simply be regarded as one more set of gods or demi-gods within a larger constellation of deities.

It is easy to see why a religion that includes angels encourages a spiritual ecology in which 'the human world rests within the wider sphere of the divine'. It remains less clear why 'taking angels seriously is a way of establishing Christian theocentrism' (van der Hart 1972, 17; Bonino 2016, 4). The compatibility of these positions comes into focus only when we recall that angels are named in a way that defines not their independent characteristics and capacities but their function, which emphasises 'the radical subordination of the angels to God' (Bonino 2016, 13). Angelologies that elaborate the nature as well of function of the angels further emphasise this subordination by insisting on their creatureliness, in contradistinction to the uncreated nature of God (Bonino 2016, 51).

To this possibility, an important survey of all the references to angel veneration in the Second Temple Jewish tradition showed there was no evidence of a fixed 'cultic devotion' to angels; angels presented no substantial conflict of interest (Stuckenbruck and North 1995).[88] Venerative language with reference to angels either figured them as exemplars for how to worship God, or else as expressions of thanksgiving to God for actions attributed to angels. In the latter

---

[87] See also Wiebe (2021, 63).
[88] For a discussion of Stuckenbruck's important study, see Hurtado (2010, 558–60).

context, the occasional angelic petition – for help, or vengeance, or protection – either explicitly included God, or else did so implicitly: angels were understood to be operating with His warrant. None of these kinds of 'angel veneration' was conceived as a substitute for, or infringement upon, the worship of one God. A firm commitment to the uniqueness of the one God, expressed both in religious rhetoric and in cultic practice, clearly 'sat easily with beliefs about powerful and exalted adjutant figures, among which principal angels were prominent, sometimes portrayed as uniquely deputized to act in God's name as God's chief agent' (Hurtado 2010, 562).

The challenge that angels present to monotheism is thereby mitigated by angelology. More than this, angelology consolidates what monotheism even means. That is the more intricate and consequential story. The presence of angels within the ancient Jewish religious imaginary not only sat 'easily' with a commitment to monotheism: angels actively augmented God's status. This counterintuitive outcome springs from the fact that 'most often the venerative language [for angels] is followed by an explanation which emphasizes the supremacy of God' (Stuckenbruck and North 1995, 201). Not only is it misleading to link 'angel veneration' in ancient Jewish religion with some alleged weakened sense of God's uniqueness: the very opposite is true (Stuckenbruck and North 1995, 202).[89]

That angels can support rather than compromise belief in a Supreme Being is a conclusion that must once more be addressed as part of the larger question of what counts as monotheism in the first place. Several observations have been made so far that relate to whether monotheism is not best understood as a distinctive category at all, but as polytheism 'in disguise'; that there is in any event no such thing as *pure* monotheism (Corbin 1981b; Versnel 2011). Some ground must be given here, but the hard line that monotheism is simply not meaningful as a term is every bit as reductive as the claim that monotheism has no shared history or sympathies with polytheism. It is less important what nomenclature is deployed to describe a given religion at a given moment in its historical development than that there is clarity on what, exactly, the operative term implies.

---

[89] For a very different but no less fascinating case, see James Adair's *History of the American Indians* (1775), which argues for how the Catawba, Cherokee, Muscogee, Choctaw and Chickasaw people of North America, supposedly descended from the lost ten tribes of Israel, conducted their belief in the ministration of angels. Whereas 'The ancient heathens, it is well known, worshipped a plurality of gods', 'these Indian Americans pay their religious devoir to Loak-Ishtōhoollo-Aba, "the great, beneficent, supreme, holy spirit of fire"': 'He is with them the sole author of warmth, light, and of all animal and vegetable life. They do not pay the least perceivable adoration to any images, or to dead persons; neither to the celestial luminaries, nor evil spirits, nor any created being whatsoever' (Adair 1775, 17–18).

It is prudent, for a start, to pause over the fact that the commonly accepted contemporary meaning of the word monotheism as belief in a single deity only emerged within European philosophical debates of the seventeenth and eighteenth centuries (MacDonald 2003, 5–21). Early Jewish, Christian, and Islamic 'monotheisms' by no means denied the existence of other divinities, but only that there was a single God superior to all others, and as such uniquely worthy of exclusive worship and obedience.[90] All three of these ancient religions accommodated beliefs about other spiritual beings – and not only false idols: divinities believed to be real. Hurtado puts the point with helpful bluntness: 'If "monotheism" were to be restricted to the belief that there is only one heavenly/divine being, then very few Jews, Christians, or Muslims have ever qualified as monotheists' (Hurtado 2010, 549).

In Judaism, it is possible to chart a double recalibration. In the postexilic period, with the development of explicit monotheism, divine beings known as the 'sons of God' who were members of the Divine Council were 'in effect demoted to what are now known as "angels", understood as beings created by God, but immortal and thus superior to humans' (Coogan 2009, 408). Then, as Christian conceptualisations of angels became increasingly powerful and pervasive, and the idea of monotheism as a defining feature of Judaism continued to harden into the twentieth century, Judaism came to forget or actively repress the extent to which angels have, as Ahuvia emphasises, 'a firm biblical and Jewish pedigree'.[91]

Scholars have coined alternative categories for capturing the modes in which a deity might be recognised. 'Henotheism' has been suggested as a way of indicating the belief in one deity presiding over others; 'monolatry', or 'intolerant henotheism', for the insistence that only one deity be worshipped. These terms may be helpful in certain contexts, but they are at odds with scholars of religion who readily speak of 'pagan monotheism' to express the idea that the many gods are all valid manifestations of some common divine essence (Hurtado 2010, 550). Equally, religions typically identified as monotheisms – Judaism, Christianity, Islam – imply a much more severe exclusivity than this, when it comes to the ways their holy books define and delimit their deity, and restrict cultic worship (Hurtado 2010, 550).

What 'monotheism' portends is crucial to understanding the place of angels, not least because they are not perfectly fungible. That angels appear in all the

---

[90] On the limitations of the term monotheism as applied to ancient religions, and Judaism and Christianity in particular, see Hurtado (2010) and Heiser (2004, 9–18).

[91] 'Twentieth-century scholarly accounts of Judaism's pure, monotheistic origins, taught in seminaries as well as the academy, have obscured the role of angels in the Bible, classical Jewish texts, and Jewish ritual practice' Ahuvia (2021, 2). See also Kaufmann (1960).

Abrahamic faiths, even at times sharing the same names, does not mean that they are identical, or play identical roles. Abraham the patriarch is considered a foundational figure to Jews, Christians, and Muslims alike, but no one would question his significance for Jewish self-understanding (Ahuvia 2021, 3); and the same point would obviously apply to Christianity and Islam too. Judaism, Christianity, and Islam do, in certain respects, construe angels differently – and they also, in certain respects, go about that construal differently too. Their angelogical traditions converge but also diverge.[92]

The point may be sharpened: that there is some commonality on angels means differences which emerge actually prove to be more illuminating. This is a variation on the principle already adduced, that the inclusion of angels within monotheism may compromise the idea of a sovereign deity only if there is insufficient clarity on the relative status of angels to God. If relativity is clear, they serve instead to promote God's unrivalled position.

'Polytheism knew spiritual hierarchies but never knew how *to distinguish and contrast* the Creator and the creation' (Bulgakov 2010, 26; italics original): Bulgakov's observation sets out the stakes. The integrity of monotheism depends on the ability to recognise an order of being, which means a bimodal appreciation of continuity as well as difference, most of all, the difference between Creator versus creation. Hence what Henry Corbin called 'le paradoxe du monothéisme': a transcendent God whose nature is, by definition, beyond human comprehension can only be understood by limited, contingent minds, if He is bridged by an immanent intermediary. Angels are that primary heurism, and angelology unavoidably necessary (Corbin 1981b). Without knowledge of angels there can be no adequate knowledge of God:

> The Angel is the Face that our God takes for us, and each of us finds his God only when he recognizes that Face. The service which we can render others is to help them encounter that Face about which they will be able to say:*Talem eum vidi qualem capere potui* ['I am able to grasp such as I have seen']. (1981a, 4)

Corbin's claim cuts in different directions, depending on how one interprets the distinctions he makes between the Abrahamic monotheisms; notably, his claim that Jewish and Christian monotheism confuses 'the uniqueness of Divinity (*Theotes*) with a singular God (*theos*) which excludes other gods (*theoi*)' (Charlesworth 1999, 41). Differences might also be observed within individual

---

[92] 'Although a great deal of speculation about angels can be found in the Babylonian Talmud, those seeking a precise definition to compare with Christian theological pronouncements will be disappointed. The rabbis did not engage in systematic angelology, and only limited coherence among their traditions may be discerned'. (Ahuvia 2021, 200).

monotheisms as they developed over the centuries, not merely in a shift from henotheism to monolatry, but in terms of how the Creator is understood in relation to creation in the broadest terms.

On this subject, there is an irony as well as a clue to be found in the historical high watermark of angelology, in the ingenuity of the scholastics working on angels which occurs at the very same moment that Western metaphysics elaborates its mode from the analogy of being to the univocity of being. The change had colossal consequences. God suddenly became 'mappable on the same set of coordinates as his creatures', Robert Barron explains: 'By admitting a simple and univocal concept of being, Scotus provided a true conceptual community between God and creature and placed the project of natural know-ledge of the divine nature on a firm epistemological footing' (Barron 2007, 193). Brad Gregory has delineated the long arc of Scotus's influence in this respect, through his writings and those of other nominalist thinkers in his wake (notably, Ockham), as 'the first step toward the eventual domestication of God's transcendence' (Gregory 2012, 37–38).

Although Gregory only mentions angels twice across the almost 600 pages of his book, and those brief references are incidental to the main argument,[93] the research that informs *The Unintended Reformation* (2012) bears significantly on the history of angels within monotheism. Nominalism, unleashed by the presumption of univocity, changes the very idea of God's purported incompre-hensibility, from what Aquinas categorises as *esse*, the act of being itself, to the Ockhamist *ens*, the notion of God as an entity. If the Supreme Being is just another 'being' in the chain of being, the supposed 'bridge' angels offer is not necessary after all; the leap may be attempted analogically, without celestial intercession.

It may be that Gregory overstates things, and that his reading of Scotus, Ockham and medieval philosophy at large is too generalised, and out of date. Richard Cross (Cross 2005, 66) makes a powerful case that whatever revolution in thought might be pinned to this period, it is more adequately understood as a wave of change. There was not one single conceptual innovation, but many cresting at around the same time. Cross emphasises also that the univocity of being in its original form was a linguistic theory, a theory about how we can use certain words in certain contexts, and in consequence only indirectly has any metaphysical significance (Cross 2005, 70–71). Cross has his sights set on the presuppositions of Radical Orthodoxy, but his findings clearly impinge on

---

[93] Gregory (2012, 99, 134): The first reference is to Paul's warning about false apostles ('Even Satan disguises himself as an angel of light' (2 Cor 11:14)); the second concerns the day of judgement ('Depart from me into the eternal fire prepared for the devil and his angels' (Mt 25:41)).

Gregory's governing thesis too, and other scholars have indeed pressed this point directly (Kilcrease 2022).

Even if Scotus's claim about univocity is merely a semantic claim, and that it does not therefore have ontological consequences, it is necessary to reckon with the fact that Scotus was misread or in any event subsequently taken up in a way which modifies how human beings and God were understood to relate to one another. The significance of the univocity of being for angelology, whether indirect, or as Gregory would have it, 'unintended', remains salient. These are deep waters, but there is no need to plumb their fullest depths to recognise that debates on the uniqueness of Divinity (*Theotes*) versus a singular God (*theos*), and the nature of God's 'being' as against Being, have transformative conse-quences for the conception of angels. The Abrahamic faiths seek to accommo-date divinity in ways that include both transcendence and immanence, and angels have, historically, been the chief promissory agents for that possibility. Angels bring what's apophatic within cataphatic reach. But in so doing, they potentially unsettle God's status as an unknowable divinity without rival, even as they indirectly clarify that ineffability and pre-eminence. Angelology is in that sense a perpetual exercise in equipoise, as Newman deftly diagnosed in his own religiously troubled lifetime:

> There have been ages of the world, in which men have thought too much of Angels, and paid them excessive honour; honoured them so perversely as to forget the supreme worship due to Almighty God. This is the sin of a dark age. But the sin of what is called an educated age, such as our own, is just the reverse: to account slightly of them, or not at all; to ascribe all we see around us, not to their agency, but to certain assumed laws of nature. (Newman 1908, 358)

Newman's complaint requires some unpacking. Look at the art and literature and the books and articles published in the nineteenth century, and it can hardly be judged an age of angel apathy. The Oxford Movement encouraged a spike in sympathy for various Catholic habits that had been largely lost in England since the Reformation, including a renewed enthusiasm for angels. Outside of specific-ally religious settings too, angels figured larger than ever in the popular imagin-ation, as reflected in the art and poetry of the Pre-Raphaelites (Stanford 2019, 268, 269–75). For Newman, though, the rising cultural popularity of angels was no compensation for the fact that they were increasingly neglected within theology, quite the opposite. Their commonness was a further expression of the debasement of their divine economy, for how they were accounted 'slightly' – trivialised, paganised, and commodified – in everything from paintings and fiction to postcards and ornamental gimcrack. Martial and male angelic beings were replaced by cute children and elegant women; aloof enforcers and fierce intercessors were overtaken by divine super-soothers, defined not according to their terrible potency but in their winsomeness and devotion to mundane wellbeing.[94]

What William Empson once sniffily observed about poetry of the period might therefore plausibly be extended to angels as well, insofar as they likewise offered an 'escape' or 'holiday' from the 'business' of life, 'especially the business of becoming Fit to Survive' – and through 'an indulgence [. . .] in beliefs the scientists knew were untrue' (Empson 1984, 39).[95] The visibility of angels within culture is certainly uneven over time. Although they may fall out of theological fashion, they may rise within the popular consciousness: a slide from theological seriousness into sentimentality. That was the nub of Newman's concern as he saw it happening around him, and a tellingly similar dynamic obtains today.[96] But Newman also looks backwards, to the dark age of angelolatry and the obverse danger of elevating angels too fully, into gods.

At its best, the study of angels exemplifies Newman's double vision, his capacity to take bearings between excesses. As a theological discipline, it is braced by opposing tensions that together aim towards truth, but which are, separately, tilted towards heresy. This Element opened by suggesting the contemporary discipline had hollowed itself out, by a turn towards fideism on the one hand, and to anthropology on the other – where both lead to error, and each is necessary to make sense of the other. Understanding angels requires faith and reason, but when either one arrogates complete authority, it misleads. The challenge is how to combine them.

There are many mutually correcting oppositions in play. Angels are similar to, but different from, humans and God, just as humans are similar to, but different from, angels and apes. Angels are worthy of our reverence, but not our worship. Angels are objective, immutable realities, but angelology itself might develop, and should. As a discipline, it may look extravagant and eristic, but that is in the end a sign of its health rather than its hopelessness, insofar as an

---

[94] See Jones (2010, 69); Stanford (2019, 274–75); Bloom (2007, 27). The re-conception of angels in the nineteenth century can be read in part as an artistic development: recovering the fat-faced cherubs or putti from the Renaissance and privileging a more immediate style, in reaction to the aesthetic conventionalities of the previous generation. But as I have argued elsewhere, there are sociological factors too: the emasculation and domestication of angels might be a response to the alienation associated with industrialized labour (harps become the new, must-have angelic accessory), and as continuous with the idealization of the Victorian home, in which women and children were frequently compared with angels, and dead children elevated to the angelic realm by default. See Hurley (2020).

[95] For a riposte to Empson's remarks on poetry as mere escapism in the nineteenth century, see Hurley (2017, Ch. 3).

[96] Even as angels within the nineteenth century were evidently being debased, they also attracted new kinds of 'honour', being associated with artistic and literary inspiration, and also as proxy figures for artists and writers earnestly grappling with their faith. See Hurley (2020).

account of angels emerges through a certain intellectual restlessness and audacity, even as that itself must be tempered by the wisdom of tradition. Pope's chastening caution, 'presume not God to scan', must be checked by the folly of presuming only to look to mankind, such that God disappears altogether.

All that has been said of the bearings, bracing, and balancing required by angelology here applies to religions at large. But it has been the burden of this Element to show that monotheism requires one further, immense feat of dialectical thinking. Belief in a single, Supreme Being must also be reconciled with the holy books that insist upon other spiritual creatures, the acceptance of which risks unravelling the very idea of a monotheism itself. The suspicion of 'disguised polytheism' recrudesces. It might therefore be tempting to downplay angelology, but it is not in the end theologically tenable to do so, nor to reduce angels to symbols and metaphors. Scripture may sometimes properly invite that anthropological move, but only to some extent – not entirely. Angels are simply too pervasive, their roles too important, for them to be parsed as nothing more than human projections. The mandate of angels within the religious cosmology depends on the certitude that they are real.

Even as angels evidently pose a threat to the idea of a single deity, they also promise to mediate the idea of what such a Supreme Being might be. So it is, Corbin observed, 'sans l'angélologie, ce qu'on appelle si facilement le monothéisme périt dans un triomphe illusoire' (Corbin 1981b, 100). The hazard angels present to the foundational doctrine of monotheism cannot be separated from the metaphysical presumption that they are a defining feature of that same doctrine.

To conclude on this note is not to close with a theological opinion that might, after all, be contested. The *longue durée* of monotheism independently ratifies angelology's ambition. Notwithstanding recurrent waves of anxiety over angelolatry, angels grew more not less significant as monotheism became dominant. They offered a way of accessing the transcendent within the immanent. Correspondingly, to borrow Newman's binoculars, decline in the standing of angels within the Abrahamic faiths today suggests a general depreciation of the metaphysical life of those faiths. Charles Baudelaire infamously quipped that the wiliest trick the devil ever pulled was to make men believe he did not exist (Baudelaire 1864).[97] Debunking the whole heavenly host may in fact have been his greater ruse.

L.D.S.

---

[97] Earlier, less well-known expressions of the same insight include Wilkinson (1836, 239–40) and Ramsey (1856, 33).

# References

Adair, James (1775). *The History of the American Indians*. London: Edward and Charles Dilly.

Adamson, Peter (2002). *The Arabic Plotinus: A Philosophical Study of the 'Theology of Aristotle'*. London: Duckworth.

(2016). Philosophical Theology. In Sabine Schmidtke, ed., *The Oxford Handbook of Islamic Theology*. Oxford: Oxford University Press, 297–312.

Ahuvia, Mika (2021). *On My Right Michael, on My Left Gabriel*. Oakland: University of California Press.

Akbar, Ali (2020). *Contemporary Perspectives on Revelation and Qur'anic Hermeneutics: An Analysis of Four Discourses*. Edinburgh: Edinburgh University Press.

Alavi, Diane Karima (2007). Pillars of Religious Faith. In Vincent J. Cornell, ed., *Voices of Islam, Vol. 1: Voices of Tradition*. London: Praeger, 5–42.

Aquinas, Saint Thomas (2006). *Summa Theologiae*, 61 Vols. Cambridge: Cambridge University Press.

Asselt, Willem J. Wan (2011). *Introduction to Reformed Scholasticism*. Grand Rapids, MI: Reformation Heritage Books.

Assmann, Jan (2007). *No avari altro Dio. Il monoteismo e il linguaggio della violenza*. Bolgna: Il Mulino.

Augustine (1996). *Teaching Christianity [De Doctrina Christiana]*, trans. Edmund Hill. New York: New York City Press.

(2000). *Expositions of the Psalms [Enarrationes in Psalmos]*, trans. Maria Boulding. New York: New York City Press.

Awn, Peter J. (1983). *Satan's Tragedy and Redemption: Iblīs in Sufi Psychology*. Leiden: Brill.

Barron, Robert (2007). *The Priority of Christ: Toward a Postliberal Catholicism*. Grand Rapids, MI: Baker Publishing Group.

Barth, Karl (1985). *Unterricht in der Christlichen Religion*, Vol. 1, ed. H. Reiffen. Zürich: TVZ.

(1991). *The Göttingen Dogmatics: Instruction in the Christian Religion*, Vol. 1, trans. G. W. Bromiley. Grand Rapids, MI: Eerdmans.

Baudelaire, Charles (7 February 1864). Le Spleen de Paris. In *Le Figaro*, 3–5. Paris.

Belloc, Hilaire (1931). On the Word Scientific. In *A Conversation with an Angel and Other Essays*. London: Jonathan Cape, 204–11.

Bettini, Maurizio (2014). *In Praise of Polytheism*. California: California University Press.

Blau, Ludwig (1906). Angelology. *Jewish Encyclopaedia*. www.jewishencyclo pedia.com/articles/1521-angelology.

Bloom, Harold (1996). *Omens of Millennium: The Gnosis of Angels, Dreams and Resurrection*. New York: Riverhead Books.

(2007). *Fallen Angels*. London: Yale University Press.

Bonino, Serge Thomas OP. (2016). *Angels and Demons: A Catholic Introduction*. trans. Michael J. Miller. Washington, DC: Catholic University of America Press.

Brown, Francis, Samuel Rolles Driver, and Charles Augustus Briggs (2000). *Hebrew and English Lexicon of the Old Testament with an Appendix of Biblical Aramaic*. Oxford: Clarendon Press.

Bulgakov, Sergil (2010). *Jacob's Ladder: On Angels*. trans. and with an introduction by Thomas Allan Smith. Grand Rapids, MI: William B. Eerdmans.

Burge, Stephen (2012). *Angels in Islam: Jalal al-Din al-Suyuti's al-Haba'ik fi akhbar al-mala'ik*. London: Routledge.

Burton, Tara Isabella (2020). *Strange Rites: New Religions for a Godless World*. New York: Public Affairs.

Charlesworth, Max (1999). Religion and Religions. *Australian Religion Studies Review*. 12.2, 28–46.

Chesterton, Gilbert Keith (1933). *St Thomas Aquinas*. New York: Sheed & Ward.

(1990). *The Collected Works of G.K. Chesterton* (Vol. 21). San Franciso, CA: Ignatius Press.

(1996). *The Man Who Was Thursday*. Oxford: Oxford University Press.

Chipman, Leigh N. B. (2002). Adam and the Angels: An Examination of Mythic Elements in Islamic Sources. *Arabica*. 49.4, 429–55.

Clulee, Nicholas (1988). *John Dee's Natural Philosophy: Between Science and Religion*. London: Routledge.

Coogan, Michael D. (2009). *A Brief Introduction to the Old Testament*. Oxford: Oxford University Press.

Corbin, Henry (1981a). A letter from Henry Corbin. In David L. Miller, ed., *The New Polytheism*. Dallas, TX: Spring, 5–12.

(1981b). *Le paradoxe du monothéisme*. Paris: l'Herne.

Cottingham, John (2015). *How to Believe*. London: Bloomsbury.

Cross, Richard (2005). Duns Scotus and Suarez at the Origins of Modernity. In Wayne J. Hankey and Douglas Hedley, eds., *Deconstructing Radical*

*Orthodoxy: Postmodern Theology, Rhetoric and Truth.* Aldershot: Ashgate, 65–80.

Damon, Maria (1997). Angelology: Things with Wings. In Peter Gibian, ed., *Mass Culture and Everyday Life.* New York: Routledge, 205–211.

Dante (2007). *Paradiso,* trans. Robin Kirkpatrick. London: Penguin.

(2018). *Convivio,* ed. and trans. by Andrew Frisardi. Cambridge: Cambridge University Press.

Davidson, Herbert A. (1992). *Alfarabi, Avicenna, and Averroes, on Intellect: Their Cosmologies, Theories of the Active Intellect, and Theories of Human Intellect.* Oxford: Oxford University Press.

Davies, John Gordon (1973). *Everyday God.* London: SCM.

Davies, Owen (2018). *A Supernatural War: Magic, Divination, and Faith during the First World War.* Oxford: Oxford University Press.

Eagleton, Terry (2014). *Culture and the Death of God.* London: Yale University Press.

Emery, Kent and Andreas Speer (2001). After the Condemnation of 1277: New Evidence, New Perspectives, and Grounds for New Interpretations. In Jan Aertsen, Kent Emery and Andreas Speer, eds., *Nach der Verurteilung von 1277 / After the Condemnation of 1277: Philosophie und Theologie an der Universität von Paris im letzten Viertel des 13. Jahrhunderts. Studien und Texte / Philosophy and Theology at the University of Paris in the Last Quarter of the Thirteenth Century. Studies and Texts.* Berlin: De Gruyter, 3–20.

Empson, William (1984). *Seven Types of Ambiguity.* London: The Hogarth Press.

Eshkevari, Mohammad Fana'i (2012). *An Introduction to Contemporary Islamic Philosophy,* trans. Mostafa Hoda'I. Edgware: MIU Press.

Ficino, Marsilio (1576). De Christiana religione [On the Christian Religion], *Opera Omnia.* Basel.

Fitzmyer, Joseph A. (1957). A Feature of Qumrân Angelology and the Angels of I Cor. XI. 10. *New Testament Studies.* 4.1, 48–58.

Flint, Valerie I. J. (1991). *The Rise of Magic in Early Medieval Europe.* Princeton: Princeton University Press.

Fox, Matthew and Rupert Sheldrake (1996). *The Physics of Angels: Exploring the Realm Where Science and Spirit Meet.* San Francisco, CA: Harper San Francisco.

French, Peter (1972). *John Dee: The World of an Elizabethan Magus.* London: Routledge and Kegan Paul.

Froelich, Karlfried (1987). Pseudo-Dionysius and the Reformation of the Sixteenth Century. In Paul Rorem, ed., *Pseudo-Dionysius: The Complete Works,* trans. Colm Luibheid. London: SPCK, 33–46.

Gallorini, Louise Claude (2021). *The Symbolic Function of Angels in the Qur'ān and Sufi Literature*. PhD. Dissertation, American University of Beirut.

Gill, Meredith Jane (2014). *Angels and the Order of Heaven in Medieval and Renaissance Italy*. Cambridge: Cambridge University Press.

Gleason, Randall C. (2003). Angels and the Eschatology of Heb 1–2. *New Testament Studies*. 49, 90–107.

Goris, Harm (2003). The Angelic Doctor and Angelic Speech: The Development of Thomas Aquinas's Thought on How Angels Communicate. *Medieval Philosophy & Theology*. 11.1, 87–105.

Gould, Stephen Jay (1997). Non-overlapping Magisteria. *Natural History*. 106, 16–22.

(1999). *Rocks of Ages: Science and Religion in the Fullness of Life*. New York: Ballantine Books.

Grant, Edward (1962). Late Medieval Thought, Copernicus, and the Scientific Revolution. *Journal of the History of Ideas*. 23.2, 197–220.

Gregory, Brad (2012). *The Unintended Reformation: How a Religious Revolution Secularized Society*. Cambridge, MA: Belknap Press.

Guessoum, Nidhal (2010). *Islam's Quantum Question: Reconciling Muslim Tradition and Modern Science*. London: I.B. Tauris.

Hachlili, Rachel (2013). *Ancient Synagogues – Archaeology and Art: New Discoveries and Current Research*. Leiden: Brill.

Haleem, M. A. S. Abdel (2008). Qur'an and Hadith. In Tim Winter, ed., *The Cambridge Companion to Classical Islamic Theology*. Cambridge: Cambridge University Press, 19–32.

Harkness, Deborah E. (1999a). Climbing Jacob's Ladder: Angelology as Natural Philosophy. In *John Dee's Conversations with Angels: Cabala, Alchemy, and the End of Nature*. Cambridge: Cambridge University Press, 98–130.

(1999b). The Colloquium of Angels: Prague, 1586. In *John Dee's Conversations with Angels: Cabala, Alchemy, and the End of Nature*. Cambridge: Cambridge University Press, 9–59.

Hawting, Gerald R. (1999). *The Idea of Idolatry and the Emergence of Islam: From Polemic to History*. Cambridge: Cambridge University Press.

Heiser, Michael S. (2004). *The Divine Council in Late Canonical and Non-Canonical Second Temple Jewish Literature*. PhD. Dissertation, University of Wisconsin.

(2015). *The Unseen Realm: Recovering the Supernatural Worldview of the Bible*. Bellingham, WA: Lexham Press.

(2018). *Angels: What the Bible Really Says About God's Heavenly Host*. Bellingham, WA: Lexham Press.

Hildegard of Bingen (1882). *Liber Vitae Meritorum*. Pitra.

Hobbes, Thomas (1651). *Leviathan*. London: Andrew Crooke.

Hurley, Michael D. (2017). *Faith in Poetry: Verse Style as a Mode of Religious Belief*. London: Bloomsbury.

(2020). The Fate of Angels in the Nineteenth Century. *Religion and Literature*. 51.3–52.1, 5–18.

Hurtado, Larry W. (2010). Monotheism, Principal Angels, and the Background of Christology. In John J. Collins and Timothy H. Lim, eds., *The Oxford Handbook of the Dead Sea Scrolls*. Oxford: Oxford University Press, 546–64.

Ibrahim, Celene (2022). *Islam and Monotheism*. Cambridge: Cambridge University Press.

Iribarren, Isabel and Martin Lenz (2008). Introduction: The Role of Angels in Medieval Philosophical Inquiry. In I. Iribarren and M. Lenz, eds., *Angels in Medieval Philosophical Inquiry: Their Function and Significance*. Aldershot: Ashgate, 1–14.

James, William (1920). *The Varieties of Religious Experience: A Study in Human Nature*. London: Longmans, Green.

Jameson, Anna (2012). *Sacred and Legendary Art*, Vol. I. Cambridge: Cambridge University Press.

Jones, David Albert (2010). *Angels: A History*. Oxford: Oxford University Press.

Josephson-Storm, Jason Ā. (2017). *The Myth of Disenchantment: Magic, Modernity, and the Birth of the Human Sciences*. Chicago, IL: Chicago University Press.

Joyce, James (2003). *A Portrait of the Artist as a Young Man*. New York: Penguin.

Karanika, Andromache (2016). Messengers, Angels, and Laments for the Fall of Constantinople. In Mary R. Bachvarova, Dorota Dutsch, and Ann Suter, eds., *The Fall of Cities in the Mediterranean: Commemoration in Literature, Folk-Song, and Liturgy*. Cambridge: Cambridge University Press, 226–51.

Kaufmann, Yehezkel (1960). *The Religion of Israel*, trans. Moshe Greenberg. Chicago, IL: Chicago University Press.

Keck, David (1998). *Angels and Angelology in the Middle Ages*. Oxford: Oxford University Press.

Kellner, Menachem (2006). *Maimonides' Confrontation with Mysticism*. Liverpool: Liverpool University Press.

Kilcrease, Jack (2022). An Intended Reformulation: Of Brad Gregory, Duns Scotus, and Early Modern Metaphysics. In James Kellerman, Alden Smith, and Carl P. E. Springer, eds., *Athens and Wittenberg: Poetry, Philosophy, and Luther's Legacy*. Leiden: Brill, 210–33.

Klein, Elizabeth (2018). *Augustine's Theology of Angels*. Cambridge: Cambridge University Press.

Knowles, Michael David OSB (1975). The Influence of Pseudo-Dionysius on Western Mysticism. In Peter Brooks, ed., *Christian Spirituality: Essays in Honour of Gordon Rupp*. London: SCM Press, 79–94.

Latour, Bruno (1991). *Nous n'avons jamais été modernes: Essai d'anthropologie symétrique*. Paris: Éditions La Découverte & Syrons.

Lenz, Martin (2008). Why Can't Angels Think Properly: Ockham against Chatton and Aquinas. In Isabel Iribarren and Martin Lenz, eds., *Angels in Medieval Philosophical Inquiry: Their Function and Significance*. Aldershot: Ashgate, 155–70.

Leo XIII, Pope (1879). *Aeterni Patris: On the Restoration of Christian Philosophy*. www.vatican.va/content/leo-xiii/en/encyclicals/documents/hf_l-xiii_enc_04081879_aeterni-patris.html.

MacDonald, Nathan (2003). *Deuteronomy and the Meaning of 'Monotheism'*. Tübingen: Mohr Siebeck.

MacIntyre, Alasdair (1990). *Three Rival Versions of Moral Enquiry: Encyclopedia, Genealogy, and Tradition*. Notre Dame, IN: University of Notre Dame Press.

Maritain, Jacques (1944). *The Dream of Descartes*. New York: Philosophical Library.

(1995). Augustinian Wisdom. In *Distinguish to Unite: The Degrees of Knowledge*, trans. Gerald B. Phelan and presented by Ralph McInerny Part 2. Notre Dame, IN: University of Notre Dame Press, 291–309.

Marrone, Steven P. (2001). Aristotle, Augustine and the Identity of Philosophy in Late Thirteenth-Century Paris: The Case of Some Theologians. In Jan Aertsen, Kent Emery, and Andreas Speer, eds., *Nach der Verurteilung von 1277 / After the Condemnation of 1277: Philosophie und Theologie an der Universität von Paris im letzten Viertel des 13. Jahrhunderts. Studien und Texte / Philosophy and Theology at the University of Paris in the Last Quarter of the Thirteenth Century. Studies and Texts*. Berlin: De Gruyter, 276–98.

Mayr-Harting, Henry (1998). *Perceptions of Angels in History: An Inaugural Lecture delivered in the University of Oxford on 14 November 1997*. Oxford: Clarendon Press.

McGilchrist, Iain (2010). *The Master and His Emissary: The Divided Brain and the Making of the Western World*. New Haven, CT: Yale University Press.

McHale, Brian (2017). Angels, Ghosts, and Postsecular Visions. In Stephen J. Burn, ed., *American Literature in Transition, 1990–2000*. Cambridge: Cambridge University Press, 32–47.

Milton, John (2000). *Paradise Lost*. London: Penguin.

Murata, Sachiko (1987). The Angels. In Seyyed Hossein Nasr, ed., *Islamic Spirituality: Foundations*. London: Routledge & Kegan Paul, 324–44.

Murdoch, John Emery (1991). Pierre Duhem and the History of Late Medieval Science and Philosophy in the Latin West. In Ruedi Imbach and Alfonso Maierù, eds., *Gli Studi di filosofia medievale fra otto e novecento*. Rome: Edizioni di storia e letteratura, 253–302.

Newman, John Henry (1870). *An Essay in Aid of a Grammar of Assent*. New York: The Catholic Publication Society.

(1878). *An Essay on the Development of Christian Doctrine*. Harmondsworth: Penguin.

(1908). Sermon 29: The Powers of Nature. *Parochial and Plain Sermons*. London: Longmans, Green.

Olyan, Saul M. (1993). *A Thousand Thousands Served Him: Exegesis and the Naming of Angels in Ancient Judaism*. Tübingen: J.C.B. Mohr.

Orsi, Robert A. (2004). *Between Heaven and Earth: The Religious Worlds People Make and the Scholars Who Study Them*. Princeton: Princeton University Press.

(2016). *History and Presence*. Cambridge, Mass: Harvard University Press.

Pannenberg, Wolfhart (1994). *Systematic Theology*, Vol. 2, trans. G. W. Bromiley. Grand Rapids, MI: Eerdmans.

Pascal, Blaise (1960). *Pensées*. trans. John Warrington. London: J.M. Dent & Sons.

Pasulka, Diana W. (2019). *American Cosmic: UFOs, Religion, Technology*. Oxford: Oxford University Press.

Peers, Glenn (2001). *Subtle Bodies: Representing Angels in Byzantium*. Berkeley, CA: University of California Press.

Percival, Henry R. (tr.) (1960). Synod of Laodicea. In Henry R. Percival, ed., *The Seven Ecumenical Councils of the Undivided Church*. Grand Rapids, MI: William B. Eerdmans, 123–60.

Perl, Eric D. (2007). *Theophany: The Neoplatonic Philosophy of Dionysius the Areopagite*. Albany, NY: State University of New York Press.

Perler, Dominik (2008). Thought Experiments: The Methodological Function of Angels in Late Medieval Epistemology. In Isabe Iribarren and Martin Lenz, eds., *Angels in Medieval Philosophical Inquiry: Their Function and Significance*. Aldershot: Ashgate, 143–54.

Philo (1929). Philo. ed. and trans. by Francis Henry Colson and George Herbert Whitaker. Loeb Classical Library, Vol. 2. Cambridge, MA: Harvard University Press.

Pinker, Steven (2018). *Enlightenment Now: The Case for Reason, Science, Humanism, and Progress*. London: Penguin.

Plato (2017). Apology. *Euthyphro; Apology; Crito; Phaedo*, ed. and trans. by Chris Emlyn-Jones and William Preddy. Loeb Classical Library. Cambridge, MA: Harvard University Press, 63–147.

Pope, Alexander (2006). Essay on Man. *Alexander Pope: The Major Works*. Oxford: Oxford University Press.

Potter, Dylan David (2017). *Angelology: Recovering Higher-Order Beings as Emblems of Transcendence, Immanence, and Imagination*. Cambridge: James Clarke.

Pseudo-Dionysius the Areopagite (1965). The Celestial Hierarchies. In *Mystical Theology and the Celestial Hierarchies*, trans. and edited by the editors of The Shrine of Wisdom. Surrey: The Shrine of Wisdom, 17–61.

Ramsey, William (1856). *Spiritualism, a Satanic Delusion, and a Sign of the Times*. Peacedale, RI: H.L. Hastings.

Reed, Annette Yoshiko (2020). *Demons, Angels, and Writing in Ancient Judaism*. Cambridge: Cambridge University Press.

Rees, Valery (2013). *From Gabriel to Lucifer: A Cultural History of Angels*. London: I. B. Tauris.

Roques, René (1958). Introduction. In Gunter Heil and Maurice de Gandillac, eds., Pseudo-Dionysius the Areopagite, *La Hiérarchie Céleste*. SC Vol. 58. Paris: Du Cerf, v–xci.

Ross, George Macdonald (1985). Angels. *Philosophy*. 60.234, 495–511.

Ruickbie, Leo (2018). *Angels in the Trenches: Spiritualism, Superstition and the Supernatural during the First World War*. London: Robinson.

Sacks, Jonathan (2015). *Not in God's Name: Confronting Religious Violence*. London: Hodder & Stoughton.

Schäfer, Peter (2018). *Mirror of His Beauty: Feminine Images of God and the Bible to the Early Kabbalah*. Princeton, TX: Princeton University Press.

Schumacher, Lydia (2023). Angels. In *Human Nature in Early Franciscan Thought: Philosophical Background and Theological Significance*. Cambridge: Cambridge University Press, 276–84.

Scribano, Emanuela (2015). Angel. In Lawrence Nolan, ed., *The Cambridge Descartes Lexicon*. Cambridge: Cambridge University Press, 16–19.

Serres, Michael (1995). *Angels: A Modern Myth*, trans. Francis Cowper. Paris: Flammarion.

Sheldrake, Rupert (2013). *The Science Delusion: Freeing the Spirit of Enquiry.* London: Hodder and Stoughton.

Smith, William Robertson. (1875). Angel. In *Encyclopaedia Britannica.* 9th edn. Vol. 2. Edinburgh: A. & C. Black, 26–28.

Sommer, Benjamin D. (2009). *The Bodies of God and the World of Ancient Israel.* Cambridge: Cambridge University Press.

Spencer, Nicholas (2023). *Magisteria: The Entangled Histories of Science and Religion.* London: Oneworld, 78–83.

Spevack, Aaron (2014). *The Archetypal Sunni Scholar: Law, Theology, and Sufism in the Synthesis of al-Bājūrī.* Albany, NY: SUNY Press.

(2018). Egypt and the Later Ash'arite School. In Sabine Schmidtke, ed., *The Oxford Handbook of Islamic Theology.* Oxford: Oxford University Press, 534–46.

Stanford, Peter (2019). *Angels: A Visible and Invisible History.* London: Hodder and Stoughton.

Stewart, Jon (2020). Feuerbach's Conception of Theology or Philosophy of Religion as Anthropology. In Peter Sajda, ed., *Modern and Postmodern Crises of Symbolic Structures.* Leiden: Brill, 79–92.

Strauss, David Friedrich (1841). *Die christliche Glaubenslehre in ihrer geschichtlichen Entwicklung und im Kampfe mit der modernen Wissenschaft dargestellt,* Vol. 2. Tubingen: Osiander.

Stroumsa, Guy G. (1983). Form(s) of God: Some Notes on Meuauron and Christ. *Harvard Theological Review.* 76.3, 269–88.

Stuckenbruck, Loren and Wendy North (1995). *Angel Veneration and Christology.* WUNT 2/70. Tübingen: Mohr Siebeck.

(2004). *Early Jewish and Christian Monotheism.* London: T&T Clark International.

Tavard, Georges (1968). *Die Engel.* Freiburg: Herder.

Taylor, Charles (2007). *A Secular Age.* Cambridge, MA: The Belknap Press of Harvard University.

Thompson, Edward Palmer (1963). *The Making of the English Working Class.* London: V. Gollancz.

Traherne, Thomas (1908). *Centuries of Meditations,* edited by Bertram Dobell. London: Bertram Dobell.

Trigg, Roger (2020). *Monotheism and Religious Diversity.* Cambridge: Cambridge University Press.

Turmel, Joseph (1898). Histoire de l'angélologie des temps apostoliques à la fin du Ve siècle. *Révue d'histoire et de littérature réligieuse.* 3, 407–34.

Tuschling, Ruth M. M. (2007). *Angels and Orthodoxy.* Tubingen: Mohr Siebeck.

van der Hart, Rob (1972). *The Theology of Angels and Devils*. Cork: Mercier.

Vedantam, Shankar and Bill Mesler (2021). *Useful Delusions: The Power and Paradox of the Self-Deceiving Brain*. New York: W. W. Norton.

Versnel, Henk S. (2011). *Coping with the Gods: Wayward Readings in Greek Theology*. Leiden: Brill.

Walker, Daniel Pickering (1975). *Spiritual and Demonic Magic: From Ficino to Campanella*. Notre Dame, IN: University of Notre Dame Press.

Watt, William Montgomery. (1994). *Islamic Creeds*. Edinburgh: Edinburgh University Press.

White, Michael (1999). *Isaac Newton: The Last Sorcerer*. Boston: Da Capo Press.

Whitman, Walt (1897). A Noiseless Patient Spider. *Leaves of Grass*. Boston: Small, Maynard.

Wiebe, Gregory D. (2021). *Fallen Angels in the Theology of St Augustine*. Oxford: Oxford University Press.

Wigner, Eugene (1960). The Unreasonable Effectiveness of Mathematics in the Natural Sciences. *Communications in Pure and Applied Mathematics*. 13.1, 1–14.

Wilkinson, John (1836). Is the Sacrifice of Christ Held in Proper Estimation by the Society of Friends? In *Quakerism Examined: In A Reply to the Letter of Samuel Tuke*. London: T. Ward, 141–250.

Wolff, Uwe (1991). *Die Wiederkehr der Engel: Boten zwischen New Age, Dichtung und Theologie*. Stuttgart: EZW.

(2007). The Angels' Comeback: A Retrospect at the Turn of the Millennium. In Friedrich V. Reiterer, Nicklas Tobias, and Karin Schöpflin, eds., *Angels: The Concept of Celestial Beings: Origins, Development and Reception*. Berlin: de Gruyter, 695–714.

Wood, Donald (2013). An Extraordinarily Acute Embarrassment: The Doctrine of Angels in Barth's Gottingen Dogmatics. *Scottish Journal of Theology Ltd*. 66.3, 319–37.

Wood, Ellen Meiksins (2012). *Liberty and Property: A Social History of Western Political Thought from the Renaissance to Enlightenment*. London: Verso Books.

Woolf, Virginia (1966). Mr Bennett and Mrs Brown. *Collected Essays of Virginia Woolf*, Vol. 1. London: The Hogarth Press, 319–37.

(1977). *The Letters of Virginia Woolf*. Vol. 3, 1923–1928, ed. Nigel Nicolson. London: Hogarth Press, 475–78.

Zwemer, Samuel M. (1937). The worship of Adam by Angels. *Muslim World*. 27, 115–27.

# Acknowledgements

This Element was first conceived at an international conference on angelology hosted in Santiago, Chile, in 2018, and I am indebted to the organiser, Felix Schmelzer, and the many brilliant participants for making the event such a stimulating occasion. Professors John Marenbon and Stephen Burge were kind enough to read an early draft of this thesis, and their many incisive suggestions and corrections were invaluable; all errors and eccentricities that remain are mine. Samuel Webb was enormously helpful with copy-editing, chasing down references, and generally bringing the manuscript up to scratch. The series editors, Paul K. Moser and Chad Meister, and CUP's anonymous reviewers, were also wonderfully supportive. I am always and endlessly grateful to my wife, Jilly, for believing in me, and to my three daughters, Natasha, Francesca, and Clemmie, whose irony at my expense is a salutary corrective to any possible excess of self-belief. Finally, I must thank the Master and Fellows of Trinity College, Cambridge, for supporting my research. This small work of large ambition is dedicated to my late mother, with whom I had many conversations about angels, and in whose good company she now rests.

Cambridge Elements ⹀

# Religion and Monotheism

## Paul K. Moser
*Loyola University Chicago*

Paul K. Moser is Professor of Philosophy at Loyola University Chicago. He is the author of *God in Moral Experience; Paul's Gospel of Divine Self-Sacrifice; The Divine Goodness of Jesus; Divine Guidance; Understanding Religious Experience; The God Relationship; The Elusive God* (winner of national book award from the Jesuit Honor Society); *The Evidence for God; The Severity of God; Knowledge and Evidence* (all Cambridge University Press); and *Philosophy after Objectivity* (Oxford University Press); coauthor of *Theory of Knowledge* (Oxford University Press); editor of *Jesus and Philosophy* (Cambridge University Press) and *The Oxford Handbook of Epistemology* (Oxford University Press); and coeditor of *The Wisdom of the Christian Faith* (Cambridge University Press). He is the coeditor with Chad Meister of the book series *Cambridge Studies in Religion, Philosophy, and Society.*

## Chad Meister
*Affiliate Scholar, Ansari Institute for Global Engagement with Religion, University of Notre Dame*

Chad Meister is Affiliate Scholar at the Ansari Institute for Global Engagement with Religion at the University of Notre Dame. His authored and co-authored books include *Evil: A Guide for the Perplexed* (Bloomsbury Academic, 2nd edition); *Introducing Philosophy of Religion* (Routledge); *Introducing Christian Thought* (Routledge, 2nd edition); and *Contemporary Philosophical Theology* (Routledge). He has edited or co-edited the following: *The Oxford Handbook of Religious Diversity* (Oxford University Press); *Debating Christian Theism* (Oxford University Press); with Paul Moser, *The Cambridge Companion to the Problem of Evil* (Cambridge University Press); and with Charles Taliaferro, *The History of Evil* (Routledge, in six volumes). He is the co-editor with Paul Moser of the book series *Cambridge Studies in Religion, Philosophy, and Society.*

## About the Series

This Cambridge Element series publishes original concise volumes on monotheism and its significance. Monotheism has occupied inquirers since the time of the Biblical patriarch, and it continues to attract interdisciplinary academic work today. Engaging, current, and concise, the Elements benefit teachers, researched, and advanced students in religious studies, Biblical studies, theology, philosophy of religion, and related fields.

Cambridge Elements $\equiv$

# Religion and Monotheism

## Elements in the Series

A full series listing is available at: www.cambridge.org/er&m